NORTH DAKOTA
a pictorial history

By David P. Gray & Gerald G. Newborg

This is number _21_ of a limited edition.

NORTH DAKOTA
CENTENNIAL
1985 North Dakota Centennial Commission

TELEVISION FIRST

(1953)

(1988)

KXMC WAS THE FIRST TELEVISION STATION IN NORTH DAKOTA, BRINGING NEWS AND ENTERTAINMENT TO THE PRAIRIE. FOR OVER 35 YEARS WE HAVE GROWN WITH NORTH DAKOTA AND WE REMAIN NUMBER ONE IN THE MINOT AREA.

SINCE OPENING IN 1953 WE HAVE BROUGHT OUR BRAND OF TELEVISION TO THE BISMARCK, DICKINSON, AND WILLISTON AREAS. WE COVER THE WESTERN HALF OF THE STATE AND WE ARE PROUD TO BE A PART OF THE RICH HERITAGE THAT IS NORTH DAKOTA.

KX13	KX12	KX11	KX2
KXMC-TV MINOT	KXMB-TV BISMARCK MANDAN	KXMD-TV WILLISTON	KXMA-TV DICKINSON

NORTH DAKOTA
a pictorial history

David P. Gray   **Gerald G. Newborg**

THE
DONNING COMPANY
PUBLISHERS
NORFOLK/VIRGINIA BEACH

*In Memory of
Larry R. Remele
1945-1988*

*unflowers ripen under a
orth Dakota sky in the Red
iver Valley. Before the land
nderwent heavy cultivation,
e Red River Valley was a
assland dominated by the
g bluestem, a native grass
at grew from four to six feet
igh. Other shorter grasses,
ch as the feather bunch
ass, slender wheat grass,
nd western wheat grass,
vered much of the Red River
alley. Courtesy of the
D. Tourism Promotion
ivision*

The second longest river in the United States, the Missouri stretches 2,315 miles from its headwaters in Montana to its mouth where it joins the Mississippi at Saint Louis. About fifty miles of natural Missouri River front remains in North Dakota. The Missouri consists of reservoirs for Garrison and Oahe dams for most of its length in the state. Courtesy of the N.D. Tourism Promotion Division

Shown here is a winter scene in the valley. The Red River Valley was formerly the bottom of Lake Agassiz, a glacial lake that disappeared about eight thousand years ago. The flatness of the land and the richness of the soil are a result of these beginnings. Courtesy of the N.D. Tourism Promotion Division

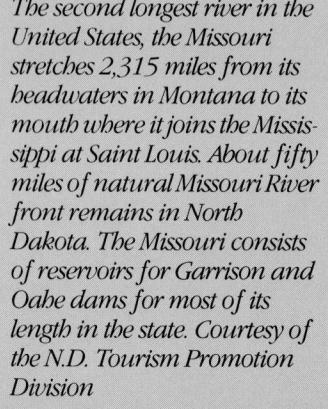

The Donning Company/Publishers
Norfolk/Virginia Beach

The Donning Company/Publishers
5659 Virginia Beach Boulevard
Norfolk, Virginia 23502

Edited by Valerie von Weich
Richard A. Horwege, Senior Editor

Library of Congress Cataloging-in-Publication Data:

Gray, David P.
    North Dakota: a pictorial history/
    by David P. Gray and Gerald G. Newborg.
    p.   cm.
    Bibliography: p.
    Includes index.
    ISBN 0-89865-726-1
    1. North Dakota—History—Pictorial works. 2. North Dakota—Description and travel—Views. I. Newborg, Gerald G. II. Title.
F637.G73   1988
978.4—dc 19   88-21906
                        CIP

Printed in the United States of America

The Turtle Mountains region is forested, with almost pure stands of oak remaining. Aspen is found in heavy groves throughout the mountain region. Only 2 percent of North Dakota is forested. *Courtesy of the N.D. Tourism Promotion Division*

Devils Lake is situated in the northeastern part of the state and is North Dakota's largest natural lake. Choice fishing, boating, sailing, camping, and historic sites attract thousands of visitors to Devils Lake. *Courtesy of the N.D. Tourism Promotion Division*

TABLE OF CONTENTS

Foreword 7

Acknowledgments 9

Introduction 11

Chapter 1
The Land and Prehistoric Peoples
  of North Dakota 13

Chapter 2
Historic Indians of North Dakota 21

Chapter 3
The Frontier: 1738-1890 49

Chapter 4
Settling North Dakota: 1870-1915 77

Chapter 5
War and Depression: 1915-1940 129

Chapter 6
War Years and New Prosperity:
  The 1940s and 1950s 159

Chapter 7
Modern North Dakota: 1960 to the Present ... 187

North Dakota Symbols 233

Chronology of North Dakota 249

Bibliography 256

Index 258

About the Authors 264

A shallow lake formed in the 1960s behind Oahe Dam near Pierre, South Dakota. The reservoir still has many trees protruding from the lake bed. Courtesy of Harold Umber, N.D. Game and Fish Department

Open prairie is pictured here in the mid-section of North Dakota. The Drift Prairie hosts shorter grasses than the Red River Valley. The dominant grass species in the Drift Prairie are the needle and thread, western wheat grass, slender wheat grass, prairie June grass, and blue grama. Courtesy of Craig Bihrle, N.D. Game and Fish Department

FOREWORD

A photographic history of North Dakota has been long awaited. It is appropriate that it appears for the centennial of North Dakota statehood. The authors have carefully selected photographs, many not previously published, which span the years of photography in the state. We can only wish the camera had been invented earlier.

Photographic images allow us to truly travel back in time to view a moment of history captured forever through the eye of the camera. A photograph is but a brief glimpse of a tiny segment of the larger world, but its enduring nature allows more detailed scrutiny of a scene than our actual presence. We can return again and again to view what our memory would distort. Photographs, too, are selective and limited in scope; but unlike written descriptions, drawings, or paintings, the information they contain is not filtered through another's mind. Each viewer can draw original conclusions and make fresh discoveries.

Enjoy your visual trip through North Dakota's past. While the captions offer guidance, each scene provides a challenge of discovery. May your journey be exciting, informative, and enriching.

James E. Sperry

Superintendent
State Historical Society of North Dakota

Rolling prairie in North Dakota's Slope region hosts grasses as well as buffalo berry shrubs, dogwood, Juneberry, wild rose, juniper, Rocky Mountain red cedar, and western yellow pine. Cottonwood flourishes in river valleys. Courtesy of the N.D. Game and Fish Department

ACKNOWLEDGMENTS

No publication of this scope is possible without the contributions and assistance of many people, most of whom are staff of the State Historical Society of North Dakota. The quality of this publication is the result of the generous contributions and support of many people involved in the preservation and interpretation of North Dakota history.

The excellence of most of the photographs throughout this book is the work of Todd Strand, photo archivist with the State Historical Society. This book would not have been possible without Todd's knowledge of the photo collections, technical expertise in the darkroom, and patience working with us. Much credit for the quality of this book goes to Todd Strand and darkroom assistant Betty Thomas. Chris Dill, Claudia Berg, and Audrey Porshe of the Museum Division generously gave information and advice on photo captions, text, and artifact selections and identification. Fern Swensen and Signe Snortland of the Archeology and Historic Preservation Division also provided assistance on photo captions and artifact selections. Reference specialists James Davis and Forrest Daniel, and Dolores Vyzralek, chief librarian of the State Archives and Historical Research Library, provided handy bits of information on a wide variety of topics. Larry Remele and staff of the Education and Interpretation Division freely supplied useful information for the project. We are grateful to James Sperry, superintendent of the Historical Society, for his encouragement in this project.

Craig Bihrle of the North Dakota Game and Fish Department made many photographs of landscape and wildlife available for this book. The North Dakota Tourism Promotion Division opened their photo files to us and made many photos available. The archives of the Roman Catholic Diocese of Bismarck also contributed several photos to this work.

The sponsors of this book deserve credit for helping to make this project possible: KXMC-TV of Minot, First American Banks of North Dakota, KXJB-TV of West Fargo, and First National Bank of Grand Forks. We also thank The Donning Company/Publishers for undertaking this project and assisting us along the way.

The time spent researching and writing this book was taken from time that should have been devoted to our families. We are grateful to them for their patience and support while this book was in preparation.

D.P.G.
G.G.N.

Buttes are large flat-topped hills rising as much as seven hundred feet above the plains. Products of water and wind erosion, buttes, such as the Killdeer Mountains in Dunn County, lend great beauty to the Slope region. Photo by David Gray

A winter scene was photographed in the Slope region. Courtesy of the N.D. Tourism Promotion Division

INTRODUCTION

Photographs are truly windows on another time, capturing moments, people, places, objects, and emotions. Photographs are historical documentation, much like old manuscripts and documents, newspapers, maps, magazines, and memorabilia. Examined closely, photographs often reveal more about their subjects than other types of historical documentation. The camera's eye takes it all in—enthusiasm, pride, or hope etched on people's faces; the hardships of homesteading and living in a sod house; the vastness and beauty of the prairie; the desperation and despair of the Great Depression; buoyant feelings at a Fourth of July parade. Photographs often provoke an emotional response within the viewer; in this lies their power and use as a means of presentation and interpretation of the past.

The authors of this volume discovered that pictorial history is a powerful and effective means to present the history of our state. Photographs and other visual documentation are an incredibly diverse source of bits of information that can be assembled together to form a panoramic mosaic that is the history of North Dakota. Like most art forms, there are limitations to the medium. Not all events in North Dakota's history were recorded photographically or pictorially. In fact, pictorial representations of the bulk of North Dakota history do not exist. The thousands of years of prehistory are recorded only through artifacts sifted from the earth. Photographs of a number of these objects appear later. The years of exploration in the eighteenth and nineteenth centuries are largely undocumented pictorially, except for the work of adventurers such as Karl Bodmer and George Catlin. Not until the invention of photo-

graphy in the 1830s and transfer of this technology to the New World do we begin to see photographic images dating from the 1860s in North Dakota. From that time, however, much of the history of North Dakota is well-documented in relative terms.

The primary source of photographs for this volume is from the photographic archives of the State Historical Society of North Dakota. In addition to still photographs, many of the images in this book are taken from motion picture film, drawings and paintings, posters, maps, leaflets, and memorabilia. Numbering some 100,000 images, the photographic archives of the State Historical Society of North Dakota are a visual storehouse of information on North Dakota. It is a treasure to the people of this state.

This pictorial history of North Dakota was commissioned in recognition of the centennial of North Dakota statehood in 1989. It is appropriate North Dakotans should celebrate their centennial by enjoying a visual history of their experiences as a community. But we should acknowledge another anniversary that occurs during our centennial year of statehood. In 1839, a Frenchman named Louis Daguerre announced the perfection of the photographic process. The invention of photography 150 years ago is an event we should also celebrate. Photography is a technology and art form that has greatly enriched our lives. It is a great tool of human progress. Without photography, much of the power and impact of the events of our past would not have been recorded. And this book would not have been possible. Enjoy now the pictorial mosaic of North Dakota history that unfolds on the following pages.

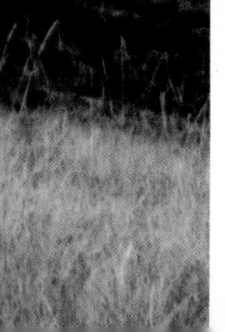

The beautiful Badlands are a dominant feature of the Slope region. The Badlands are regions that have been worn into steep hills and deep gullies by wind, rain, and flood action. Called the "Badlands" because the land is poor for farming and difficult to travel across, many still believe the name comes from the wild character of the miners, hunters, and adventurers who lived there during the frontier period. Courtesy of the N.D. Tourism Promotion Division

1

THE LAND AND PREHISTORIC PEOPLES OF NORTH DAKOTA

To understand the history of North Dakota, it is necessary to know the physical and natural setting of the land. Only by knowing of natural, physical, and climatic conditions can we begin to appreciate the challenge faced by the earliest inhabitants and historic Indian peoples, as well as later European and American settlers to live in the land that is now North Dakota.

The Land

The geographic center of North America is in North Dakota in the north central part of the state near the city of Rugby. The geographic center of the United States is in South Dakota. North Dakota is approximately 1,500 miles from the Atlantic, the Pacific, the Gulf of Mexico, and the Arctic Archipelago of North America. To the north of North Dakota are the Canadian provinces of Manitoba and Saskatchewan. To the east is Minnesota, to the west is Montana, and to the south, our sister state South Dakota. Except for the boundary with Minnesota, the Red River of the North and the Bois de Sioux, all North Dakota boundaries are straight lines, politically devised without regard to physical feature.

North Dakota is a rectangular region covering 70,837 square miles, ranking seventeenth in size among the United States. North to south, North Dakota measures 210 miles, and east to west an average of 335 miles. Before American and European settlement of North Dakota, only 2 percent of the land was covered by forests and the rest by grassland. Today there are 1,208 square miles of water surface in North Dakota with 609 square miles occupying Lake Sakakawea.

The face of North Dakota was shaped by a series of glaciations over the last million years. The last glacier, retreating some thirteen thousand years ago, covered all of North Dakota except the southwest corner. Called the Wisconsin glacier, it measured from three hundred to one thousand feet thick. The leveling action of glaciation as well as the presence of a number of large glacial lakes accounts for the relative flatness of much of North Dakota. Glaciation also affected the drainage pattern in North Dakota. A continental divide lies across the state. As a result, the Missouri River and its tributaries drain to the south, while the Red River and its tributaries flow to the north toward Hudson Bay.

North Dakota lies within two large land regions in the United States. Divided diagonally, the northeastern half of the state is part of the central lowlands stretching east to the Appalachian Moun-

American bison, more commonly known as buffalo, live within the Theodore Roosevelt National Park. Only bare remnants of the vast herds remain. Writing in 1801, Alexander Henry marveled over a herd near Park River, "The ground was covered at every point of the compass, as far as the eye could reach, and every animal was in motion." Courtesy of the N.D. Tourism Promotion Division

Lightening splits a clouded sky over the Badlands. Courtesy of Edward Bry, N.D. Game and Fish Department

tains and south to the coastal plain on the Gulf Mexico. The southwestern half of the state, star ing roughly at the Missouri River, is part of the Great Plains, rising westward to the Rocky Mou tains and extending north and south into Cana and north Texas. Traveling east to west in Nortl Dakota, one begins at 750 feet above sea level Pembina and rises to 3,000 on the plains. The land surface resembles three broad steps from east to west, rising nearly a half-mile in altitude The major land features of North Dakota are th Red River Valley in the east, the Drift Prairie ma ing up much of the central area of the state, an the Slope in the west.

The lowest step is the fertile, floorlike Red River Valley. The Valley is not a river valley, but the bottom of a portion of a vast glacial lake, La Agassiz. In North Dakota the Lake Agassiz Plain approximately thirty-five miles wide and varies 790 to 970 feet above sea level. The channel of the Red River of the North meanders and oxbc northward, flowing to Hudson Bay. The North Dakota tributaries of the Red River are the Sheyenne, Bois de Sioux, Wild Rice, Elm, Goos Turtle, Forest, Park, and Pembina rivers. The Re River Valley is broken only by the Pembina Hil in the northwest corner of the Valley rising son three hundred to five hundred feet above the surrounding land. The Red River Valley hosts a

Elk inhabit the Badlands region of North Dakota. Members of the deer family, bull elk stand about five feet at the shoulder and may weigh from 700 to 1,200 pounds. Elk usually eat grasses, but also eat twigs, juniper needles, and many hardwood trees and shrubs. Courtesy of the N.D. Tourism Promotion Division

A great blue heron is sustained by a North Dakota wetland. The more common white heron frequents North Dakota also. Courtesy of Craig Bihrle, N.D. Game and Fish Department

eep layer of humus. The soil enriched by the eep humus layer has produced some of the chest agricultural land in the world. The Valley as been so extensively cultivated that little of the riginal prairie remains.

The Drift Prairie lies between the Missouri ver and the Red River Valley. Glacial deposits, or rift, give the Drift Prairie its name. The Drift airie is an area of gently rolling hills cut by eam valleys containing thousands of potholes sloughs seasonally harboring large populations wildfowl. A large portion of the migratory bird ntral flyway passes over the Drift Prairie. The rift Prairie's soils are of glacial drift origin with e richest soil in the Lake Souris Plain. Soils roughout the rest of the Drift Prairie are lighter, inner, and rockier. Like the Red River Valley, the rift Prairie region is a grassland.

The Drift Prairie is interrupted by the Turtle Mountains and the Lake Souris Plain in the north, the Devils Lake region in the northeast, and the Missouri Escarpment. The Turtle Mountains in Rolette and Bottineau counties are a rolling, glaciated plateau rising four hundred to six hundred feet above the surrounding plains. The original peaks experienced glaciation and are buried under one hundred to two hundred feet of glacial debris. Numerous lakes in the region make the Turtle Mountains a favorite summer vacation area. The Lake Souris Plain is situated in half a dozen counties in north central North Dakota and measures approximately 170 by 70 miles. The Lake Souris Plain was the bed of a large glacial lake and is flatter than the surrounding prairie. Devils Lake is the largest natural lake in North Dakota. In origin, Devils Lake was also a glacial lake but is

The lynx is native to North Dakota. Smaller than the bobcat, the lynx preys on rabbits, rodents, foxes, small deer, and occasionally sheep and chickens. Lynxes have large feet that enable them to walk efficiently over snow. Courtesy of N.D. Tourism Promotion Division

Prairie dogs are a common sight in North Dakota. The prairie dog is a member of the squirrel family and gets its name from its shrill bark. Prairie dogs live in communities called "prairie dog towns." Courtesy of the N.D. Tourism Promotion Division

now highly saline. The lakeshore is irregular and is surrounded by high, heavily wooded morainic hills. The Missouri Escarpment lies along the western boundary of the Drift Prairie and rises some three hundred to five hundred feet above the prairie. The escarpment marks the North Dakota edge of the high plains of the western United States.

The Slope region, or Missouri Plateau to some North Dakotans, lies south and west of the Missouri and covers the southwestern half of North Dakota. Escaping much of the last glaciation, the Slope area is different from the rest of North Dakota. Though the area is hilly, it is cultivated and used for cattle grazing. Rough valleys and buttes break up the flatness of the Plains. A large part of the Williston Basin lies in western North Dakota. Thus the land is rich with mineral deposits, especially oil.

Many beautiful features accent the Slope region. A narrow band of lowlands called the Missouri Breaks follows the sweep of the Missouri River. The Missouri River, a dominant feature of the state, drains about 60 percent of North Dakota. The Missouri River has five major tributaries in North Dakota: the Yellowstone, the Little Missouri, the Knife, the Heart, and the Cannonball. The James River joins the Missouri near

nkton, South Dakota. The Killdeer Mountains
i Dunn County are two flat-topped buttes
:arred by erosion and heavily forested with
irch, oak, and cedar. The Badlands of the Little
issouri River lie in the southwest. This strip of
ugh and strangely beautiful land is 6 to 20 miles
ide and about 190 miles long. The Badlands is a
indstone, shale, and clay valley where wind and
ater have scarred and carved rock formations. A
olorful network of canyons, ravines, and gullies
over the region. Lake Sakakawea, the reservoir
ehind Garrison Dam on the Missouri River, is
ie largest lake in North Dakota and the largest
nan-made lake wholly within one state. Lake
ikakawea offers many recreational advantages to
isitors and North Dakotans alike. Lake Oahe,
cated forty miles south of Bismarck, is a reser-
oir created by Oahe Dam on the Missouri near
erre, South Dakota.

The climate of North Dakota can be consid-
ed a study in extremes. Summer days in North
akota are generally bright, clear, and pleasant.
orth Dakota has more hours of sunshine than
iy other state, shining more than fifteen hours
day from mid-May until the end of July. Even the
ottest summer days are seldom uncomfortable
ecause the humidity is usually low. Winter
eather can be severe with zero temperatures
ommon. Biting winds that sweep across the
pen plains make the cold even more bitter. July
mperatures average sixty-nine degrees in the
orth and seventy-two degrees in the south. The
ate's record high temperature was 124 degrees
Medora on September 3, 1912. January temper-
ures average three degrees in the northeast and
urteen degrees in the extreme southwest. The
ate's lowest temperature, minus sixty degrees,
as recorded at Parshall on February 15, 1936.
orth Dakota is a semiarid state. The southeast
as the most precipitation, about eighteen inches
year. Some western areas receive only about
fteen inches. Snowfall averages about thirty-two
iches yearly.

Native animal life in North Dakota included
inety-four native mammals. The most important
iammals to people in North Dakota were the
ison that migrated over the plains in herds
umbering in the hundreds of thousands. It was
ie bison that sustained many North Dakota
idians and the magnet that attracted European
nd American fur traders to the region. Hunted to
ear extinction, small herds of bison are now
ound only in parks and zoos. Other large mam-
ials are native to North Dakota, including deer,
ntelope, moose, and Audubon sheep. Fur
earers such as the mink, beaver, otter, martin,
nd fisher are native to the state. Large predators
ich as the black and grizzly bear, bobcat, lynx,
iountain lion, wolf, coyote, and red and gray
oxes are also native to North Dakota. Smaller
nimals including the weasal, skunk, and raccoon
re also present. The prairie dog is perhaps the
iost famous native of North Dakota. The sloughs,
ikes, and streams of North Dakota support

thousands of migratory wildfowl, such as ducks,
geese, pelicans, gulls, grebes, and egrets. Prairie
chickens, sage hens, sharp-tailed grouse, glovers,
western meadowlarks, as well as predatory birds
such as hawks, owls, and eagles are native to
North Dakota.

Early Peoples of North Dakota

People have inhabited North Dakota for a very
long time. The first people to live in what is now
North Dakota were probably descended from the
peoples who migrated from Siberia to Alaska over
a land bridge during the Ice Age some twenty
thousand years ago. Others may have crossed the
land bridge into North American even earlier. The
land bridge disappeared some ten thousand
years ago as the glaciers retreated, melted, and
caused the ocean levels to rise, flooding much of
what previously was dry land. The new inhabitants of North America migrated southward, eventually covering all of the Americas.

The earliest human inhabitants in North
Dakota may have arrived as long as 13,000 years
ago; archaeological evidence shows that people
were living here some 12,600 years ago. The
beginnings of human habitation in North Dakota
is referred to as the Early Prehistoric Period, lasting from 17,000 B.C. to 6000 B.C. The people of
this time are called Paleo-Indians. They were
hunters and gatherers and pursued big game
such as the giant bison and the mammoth. They
used stone tools and are especially known for
their distinctive stone spearpoints made for hunting. The Paleo-Indians were undoubtedly
nomadic and were few in number. Nothing is
known about their social or family lives, how they
looked, or the kinds of homes they made.

The Paleo-Indians were followed by a group
called Archaic Indians. The Archaic Indians lived
in North Dakota during the Middle Prehistoric
Period from 6000 B.C. to A.D. 900. The Archaic
peoples may have descended from the Paleo-
Indians and developed into peoples of later
periods, but evidence is lacking. The Archaic
peoples were also hunters and gatherers. They
hunted big game also, though the mammoth and
giant bison were by now extinct. The Archaic
peoples were nomadic and made a more sophisticated array of tools from stone and bone. They
placed their dead on raised platforms or buried
them under low piles of rocks. They may have
lived in tipis with depressed floors as suggested
by a site dating from this time in southwestern
North Dakota. They used the atlatl, or spear-
thrower. The atlatl enabled the Archaic hunters to
throw spears harder and farther, making them
more efficient hunters.

About two thousand years ago another Indian
group appeared in North Dakota. Called the
Woodland peoples, they too were hunters and
gatherers, but had many other skills and tools
their predecessors did not. The Woodland peoples practiced agriculture, made and used pottery

*This stem point dates from the
time of the earliest human
habitation in North Dakota,
circa 10,000 B.C. to 4000 B.C.
The Paleo-Indians hunted
gigantic animals such as the
mammoth and the giant
bison with spears or darts
tipped with stone points such
as this. Courtesy of the SHSND*

*This atlatl weight dates from
the Archaic or Middle Prehistoric Period, 6000 B.C. to
A.D. 900. The atlatl, or dart
thrower, was a tool that
enabled hunters to throw
spears harder and farther.
Atlatls were weighted to increase and balance the force
of the hunter's throw. This
atlatl weight is carved from
catlinite, a soft stone. Courtesy
of the SHSND*

cm
in

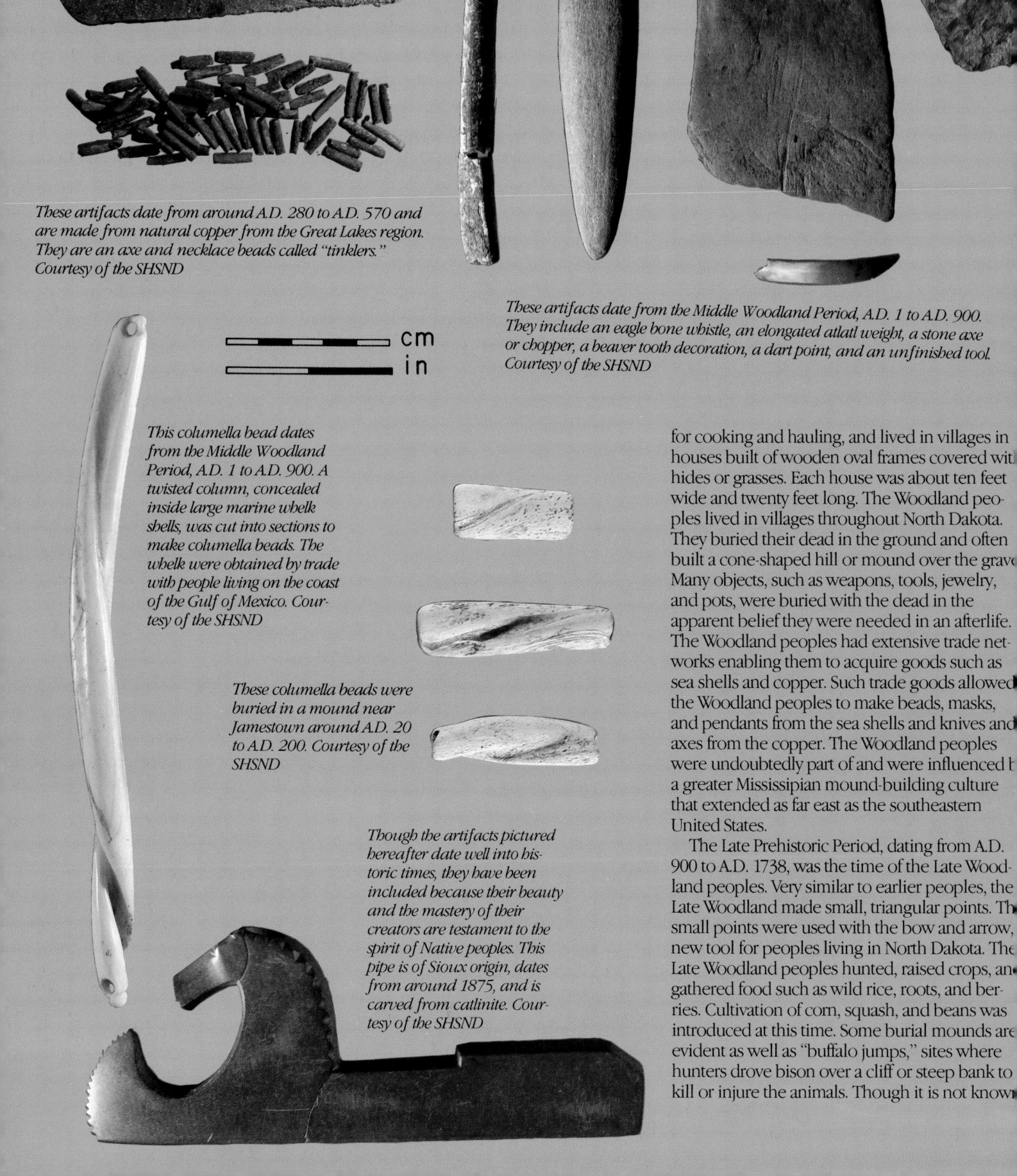

These artifacts date from around A.D. 280 to A.D. 570 and are made from natural copper from the Great Lakes region. They are an axe and necklace beads called "tinklers." Courtesy of the SHSND

These artifacts date from the Middle Woodland Period, A.D. 1 to A.D. 900. They include an eagle bone whistle, an elongated atlatl weight, a stone axe or chopper, a beaver tooth decoration, a dart point, and an unfinished tool. Courtesy of the SHSND

cm
in

This columella bead dates from the Middle Woodland Period, A.D. 1 to A.D. 900. A twisted column, concealed inside large marine whelk shells, was cut into sections to make columella beads. The whelk were obtained by trade with people living on the coast of the Gulf of Mexico. Courtesy of the SHSND

These columella beads were buried in a mound near Jamestown around A.D. 20 to A.D. 200. Courtesy of the SHSND

Though the artifacts pictured hereafter date well into historic times, they have been included because their beauty and the mastery of their creators are testament to the spirit of Native peoples. This pipe is of Sioux origin, dates from around 1875, and is carved from catlinite. Courtesy of the SHSND

for cooking and hauling, and lived in villages in houses built of wooden oval frames covered with hides or grasses. Each house was about ten feet wide and twenty feet long. The Woodland peoples lived in villages throughout North Dakota. They buried their dead in the ground and often built a cone-shaped hill or mound over the grave. Many objects, such as weapons, tools, jewelry, and pots, were buried with the dead in the apparent belief they were needed in an afterlife. The Woodland peoples had extensive trade networks enabling them to acquire goods such as sea shells and copper. Such trade goods allowed the Woodland peoples to make beads, masks, and pendants from the sea shells and knives and axes from the copper. The Woodland peoples were undoubtedly part of and were influenced by a greater Mississipian mound-building culture that extended as far east as the southeastern United States.

The Late Prehistoric Period, dating from A.D. 900 to A.D. 1738, was the time of the Late Woodland peoples. Very similar to earlier peoples, the Late Woodland made small, triangular points. The small points were used with the bow and arrow, a new tool for peoples living in North Dakota. The Late Woodland peoples hunted, raised crops, and gathered food such as wild rice, roots, and berries. Cultivation of corn, squash, and beans was introduced at this time. Some burial mounds are evident as well as "buffalo jumps," sites where hunters drove bison over a cliff or steep bank to kill or injure the animals. Though it is not known

This shell mask was found near Devils Lake and dates from around A.D. 1200 to A.D. 1500. It is made from the exterior wall of conch shells from the Gulf of Mexico and has been shaped and carved to represent a face. Carved geometric patterns may represent facial painting or tattooing. The artifact's material and style are extremely rare on the Northern Plains. Courtesy of the SHSND

This pipe is Yanktonai Sioux, dates from around 1875, and is carved from catlinite. Courtesy of the SHSND

This pipe is Sioux or possibly Chippewa and dates from around 1900. It is also carved from catlinite. Courtesy of the SHSND

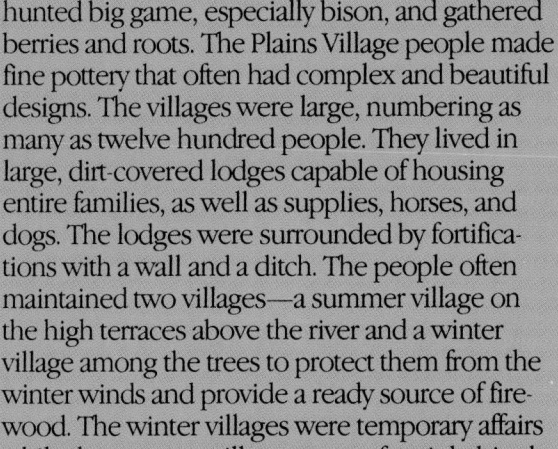

...r sure, the Late Woodland peoples may have ...en the ancestors of the Assiniboine and Chip-...ewa tribes. Other groups of Late Woodland ...eoples moved into North Dakota later, including ...e Dakota.

Other groups of Indians lived in North Dakota ...ring the Late Prehistoric Period. The Plains ...omadic peoples ranged throughout North ...kota. They were hunter-gatherers and lived in ...all bands. Sometimes the bands grouped ...gether to hunt. They hunted the huge bison ...rds that existed on the plains. They traveled ...nstantly, did not make pottery, and lived in ...is. Tipi rings, or circles of large stones used to ...ld down the edges of the tipis, can be found all ...er North Dakota. Also found are "buffalo ...mps" and flint quarries for making arrow points ...d other tools, and for trade. The Plains Nomads ...ually placed their dead on scaffolds. Tribal ...entities are difficult to determine. It is likely the ...ins Nomads were ancestors of the Dakota, ...siniboine, Crow, Cheyenne, and possibly the ...apahoe and the Blackfoot.

The third group of people living in North ...kota during the Late Prehistoric Period were ...e Plains Village people. Many of the Plains ...llage people's sites were located along the ...ssouri River. They lived in permanent villages ...d raised crops. The earliest known place where ...rn was found in North Dakota is in a village site ...Sioux County dating from A.D. 1077. Garden ...ols such as the scapula hoe appeared. Other ...ps such as beans, squash, sunflowers, and

tobacco were raised in the river valley. They hunted big game, especially bison, and gathered berries and roots. The Plains Village people made fine pottery that often had complex and beautiful designs. The villages were large, numbering as many as twelve hundred people. They lived in large, dirt-covered lodges capable of housing entire families, as well as supplies, horses, and dogs. The lodges were surrounded by fortifications with a wall and a ditch. The people often maintained two villages—a summer village on the high terraces above the river and a winter village among the trees to protect them from the winter winds and provide a ready source of firewood. The winter villages were temporary affairs while the summer villages were often inhabited for many years. The people built eagle trap pits and quarried flint. They traded widely like other Indian groups of this period. Flint from North Dakota quarries has turned up in sites as far away as Texas, Idaho, Alberta, and Wisconsin. The Plains Village people are the ancestors of the Mandan and Hidatsa people.

The Prehistoric Period of North Dakota history ends with the explorations of Pierre Gaultier de Varennes, the Seiur de La Verendrye in 1738. Before that time, however, trade goods such as cloth, metal, and glass preceded the first Europeans by many years. These trade goods and subsequent white contacts changed the Indians' way of life.

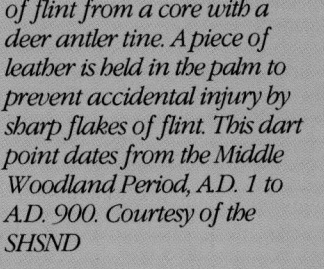

The method for making a dart point is demonstrated by an archaeologist. The point is made by pressure-flaking bits of flint from a core with a deer antler tine. A piece of leather is held in the palm to prevent accidental injury by sharp flakes of flint. This dart point dates from the Middle Woodland Period, A.D. 1 to A.D. 900. Courtesy of the SHSND

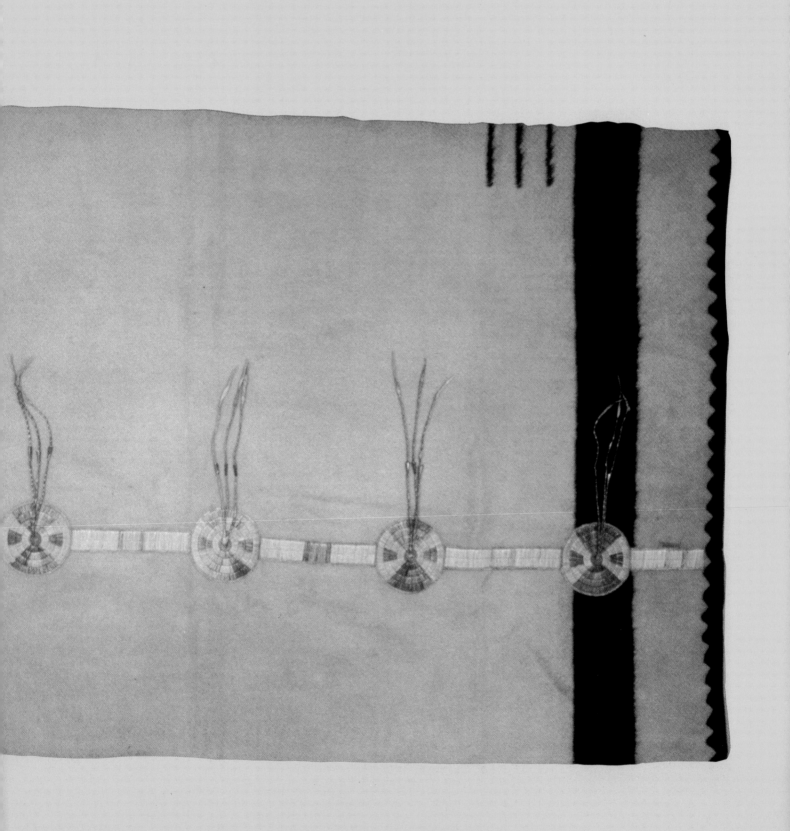

2

HISTORIC INDIANS OF NORTH DAKOTA

The various lifestyles of Indians in North Dakota reflected their efforts to adapt to life in a semi-arid region. After 1738, increasing contact with Europeans, Americans, and the federal government forced North Dakota Indians to change and adapt to a new world.

Many different and distinctive Indian cultures were present in what is now North Dakota when La Verendrye and party first visited in 1738. As we have seen, the lifestyles and traditions of native peoples are complex as well as ancient. An overview of the historic Indian presence in North Dakota should start with one of the first tribes to be identified in the historical and archaeological record, the Mandan.

The Mandan, Hidatsa, and Arikara

The people who eventually became known as the Mandan migrated to North Dakota about the year A.D. 1000. They originated in the plains of southern Minnesota and northern Iowa and settled in South Dakota. They slowly made their way north along the Missouri River and by the mid-1700s had built nine villages at the mouth of the Heart River. In 1781, a smallpox epidemic nearly wiped out the Mandan people. So few were left that they lived in only two villages. They later moved north to live closer to the Hidatsa people near the Knife River. Another smallpox epidemic in 1837 practically ended the Mandan by reducing their numbers from perhaps 2,500 to fewer than 250. Other Indian peoples were ravaged by smallpox epidemics also.

The Hidatsa people moved into North Dakota and lived in the area of Devils Lake. Around 1600 they were pressured by the Chippewa and started moving to the Missouri and eventually settled near the Mandan people. By the time Lewis and Clark visited in 1804, the Hidatsa numbered around two thousand.

The Arikara were the latest arrivals in North Dakota. Originally part of the Pawnee Nation (they called themselves Sahnish, meaning "people"), the Arikara split from their Pawnee brothers and began moving up the Missouri River. They were living in earth lodges near the mouth of the Cheyenne River in South Dakota by the mid-1700s. The Arikara were involved in a bloody war with the Teton Sioux during the late 1700s. They moved northward into North Dakota around 1792 and settled near the Cannonball River. The Arikara later joined the Mandan and Hidatsa near the mouth of the Knife River around 1825. The Arikara numbered approximately 2,800 people at

This Crow blanket dates from between 1865 to 1885. Wool blankets were fur trade items replacing traditional hide robes after decimation of the bison herds. The three points indicate the number of pelts traded for the blanket. This blanket and the objects pictured hereafter are from the Burdick Collection at the State Historical Society of North Dakota. Courtesy of the SHSND

This Sioux war shirt dates from between 1875 to 1900, and is made of muslin, quillwork, buckskin, and horsehair. Courtesy of the SHSND

This Sioux pipe bag is made of buckskin, quillwork, and beads, and dates from between 1880 to 1910. Courtesy of the SHSND

this time.

The Mandan, Hidatsa, and Arikara joined forces because disease, expecially smallpox, nearly exterminated them. An uneasy, but eventually friendly cooperation resulted from the association. Together they became known as the Three Affiliated Tribes.

Following the smallpox epidemic, the Mandan and Hidatsa moved to the south bend of the Knife River and built Like-A-Fishhook-Village in 1844. In 1862, the Arikara joined them and built Star Village across the river from Like-A-Fishhook-Village. Despite their differences (quarrels between the Mandan/Hidatsa and the Arikara often resulted in heated confrontations), the three tribes had much in common. They lived in permanent villages along the Missouri River Valley and farmed, as well as hunted bison and other game, and gathered wild foodstuffs. They raised corn, pumpkins, squash, beans, sunflowers, and tobacco. Each family worked a parcel of land. The women and children did most of the farm work.

Historically, the Three Affiliated Tribes lived in permanent villages of mound-like lodges. Lodges were constructed of log frames covered by brush, grass, and clay. The lodges were circular and measured twenty to forty feet in diameter. The ceiling had an opening for light which also served as a vent for smoke. The villages were

fortified with palisades and ditches. The Three Tribes made exquisite pottery and were skilled i basket weaving.

The Three Affiliated Tribes were governed by elected chiefs: a war chief and a village chief. A complex of clan relationships comprised the social milieu in which the people lived. Clan rel tionships often determined social position. The religious beliefs of the Three Tribes were similar to those of other Plains Indians. They believed in a Great Spirit that was present in all things, and the Mother Corn, who was sent by the Great Spir as a messenger. Life after death would be happy and dead spirits returned to the past and lived in the old villages. The Mandan celebrated the Okipa, a four-day celebration similar to the Sun Dance. The Okipa reenacted the beginnings of the Mandan people.

The Sioux

The Sioux people migrated from the east beginning in the sixteenth century. By the 1600s they settled around the forest and lake country o Lake Superior. Eventually forced out by the Chip pewa who were allied with the French, the Siou people migrated south and west. By this time, th Great Sioux Nation consisted of some twenty-six thousand people divided into three major group

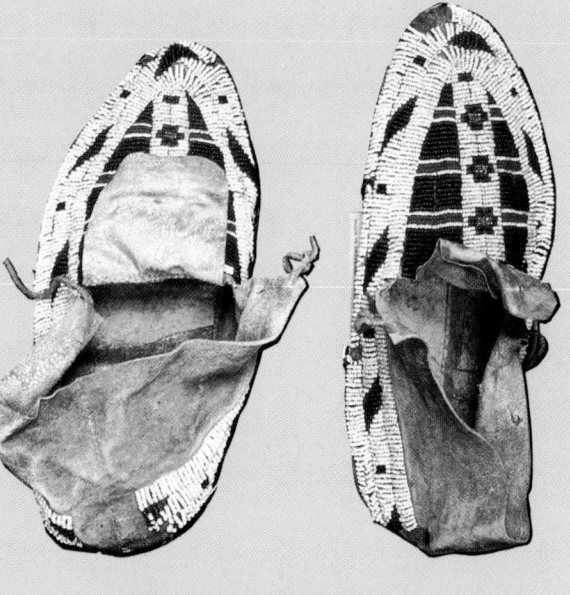

...ased on dialect and other minor cultural differences: the Dakota, the Nakota, and the Lakota.

The Dakota, or Santee Sioux, remained woodland Indians and lived mostly in Minnesota. They consisted of four tribes: the Mdwakantowan, the Wahpekute, the Sisseton, and the Wahpeton.

The Nakota, or Yankton Sioux, were larger in numbers and stature than the Dakota. They lived in the valleys of the James and Big Sioux rivers in South Dakota. The Yankton and the Yanktonai tribes made up the Nakota. They too retained many woodland Indian ways, living in permanent houses and raising corn and squash. Both groups hunted bison.

The Lakota, or Teton Sioux, was the largest and most powerful group in both stature and numbers. Adapting to a nomadic lifestyle, the Teton Sioux ranged widely, hunting bison on the Dakota plains and as far south as Oklahoma and north into Canada. The Teton consisted of seven major tribes. The Oglala, the largest tribe, lived in Wyoming, Nebraska, and western South Dakota; the Sicangu or Brules lived in Nebraska and southwestern South Dakota; and the Miniconjou, Oohenonpas, Hunkpapa, Sihasapa or Blackfoot, and the Itazipcho, who lived north of the Brule. By the mid-1700s, the Teton had reached the Missouri River driving out many other tribes, including the Cheyenne, Iowa, Otoe, and Arikara.

These Sioux moccasins are made of deerhide, beads, and parfleche, and date from between 1880 to 1900. Courtesy of the SHSND

Sioux women made finely quilled and beaded baby carrier hoods in which to wrap their infants. This baby carrier hood is made of buckskin, quillwork, beads, feathers, and cloth, and dates from between 1900 to 1930. Courtesy of the SHSND

23

Black Buffalo and Long Knife were of the Arikara tribe. Originally part of the Pawnee Nation, the Arikara split from their Pawnee brothers and began moving up the Missouri. They were locked in a bloody war with the Teton Sioux during the late 1700s and forced northward into North Dakota. The Arikara later joined the Mandan and Hidatsa near the mouth of the Knife River around 1825. After joining forces, the Mandan, Hidatsa, and Arikara were (and still are) known as the Three Affiliated Tribes. Courtesy of the SHSND

This Sisseton Sioux boy's jacket is made of buckskin, quillwork, and cloth, and dates from between 1880 to 1900. Artistic liberties were taken with the American flag. The flag was viewed as a colorful new design motif easily adapted to existing Indian arts. Courtesy of the SHSND

The Teton Sioux lived in tipis and were dependent on the bison for food and many other uses. The women owned and were responsible for the tipi; the men hunted and were warriors. The Teton gathered other foods and followed the bison herds. After acquiring horses, the Teton were able to more efficiently exploit the vast bison herds on the plains. The Teton Sioux developed a warrior society to compete and war against the other Great Plains tribes.

The Sioux elected tribal leaders to govern the people. The Teton tribal leaders gathered each summer at a meeting called the Seven Council Fires to discuss important matters. The Sioux believed in a Great Spirit that was present in the earth, sky, moon, and rock. They believed in good and evil powers that struggled for mastery of the universe. The Sioux placed their dead on scaffolds rather than bury them. Each tribe had holy men that practiced their rituals and had knowledge of tribal legends. The most important religious event of the Sioux was the Sun Dance. Lasting for twelve days during the summer, the Sun Dance was a means of asking the Great Spirit to provide a bountiful and meaningful life, and was performed by the men. Dancers who danced "Gaze at the Sun Buffalo" had wooden pins placed through their back shoulders with two to four bison skulls attached. Dancers who danced "Gaze at the Sun Staked" were placed in the center of four upright poles with ropes attached from each pole to wooden pins in the dancer's chest and back. The "Gaze at the Sun Suspended" saw dancers hanged from the poles suspended by cords and pins attached to their breasts.

The Chippewa

The Chippewa or Ojibwa people moved west from the Saint Lawrence River Valley in Canada in advance of white settlers and traders, and by the 1600s were in the area around Lake Superior. The Chippewa were traders, often acting as middlemen between the French and other Indian tribes. The Chippewa dominated Wisconsin and fought a forty-four-year war with the Santee Sioux. In 1780 the Chippewa and their allies, the French, Cree, and Assiniboine, defeated the Santee in a great battle at Saint Croix Falls, Wisconsin. The Chippewa claimed all of Minnesota and Wisconsin as their hunting grounds. Fur trappers and traders, the Chippewa ranged west from the Red River to the Souris River in north central North Dakota. The Chippewa that made this region their home after the 1790s had to adapt to a life on the plains. The Plains Chippewa became nomads, following the bison herds. They established a permanent band near Pembina in the early 1800s where Alexander Henry had established a trading post. They soon became known as the Turtle Mountain Band.

The blood brothers of the Chippewa, the Métis (French for "mixed"), were part French and part Indian. The Métis developed a distinct culture—a blend of French language and traditions and Indian language and culture, and lived alongside the Chippewa. The Métis developed the famous Red River Cart and were responsible for opening trade between Pembina and Saint Paul.

Hunting bison on the plains brought the Chippewa into conflict with the Sioux and in an

The Real Site of FishHook no.3 VilLage, 1834-1886.
Drawn by Martin BearsArm.

Like-a-Fishhook-Village was established by the Hidatsa and the Mandan in 1844. The village was so named for a bend in the Missouri River. Earth lodge villages, each of which may have had as many as twelve hundred residents, were organized in no particular pattern. Villages were fortified with palisades and ditches. In 1862 the Arikara built Star Village across the river from Like-A-Fishhook-Village, but later joined the Mandan and Hidatsa at Like-A-Fishhook-Village. Courtesy of the SHSND

A Hidatsa winter village, circa 1833-1834, was depicted by Karl Bodmer. The winter villages were situated in wooded areas for protection from the winds, and to provide a ready source of firewood. Winter villages were only temporary while the summer villages were more permanent. Courtesy of the SHSND

A Hidatsa camp was photographed at the Fort Berthold Indian Reservation. The Hidatsa lived in earth lodges like the Mandan, though this pair are pictured in a tipi camp. Courtesy of the SHSND.

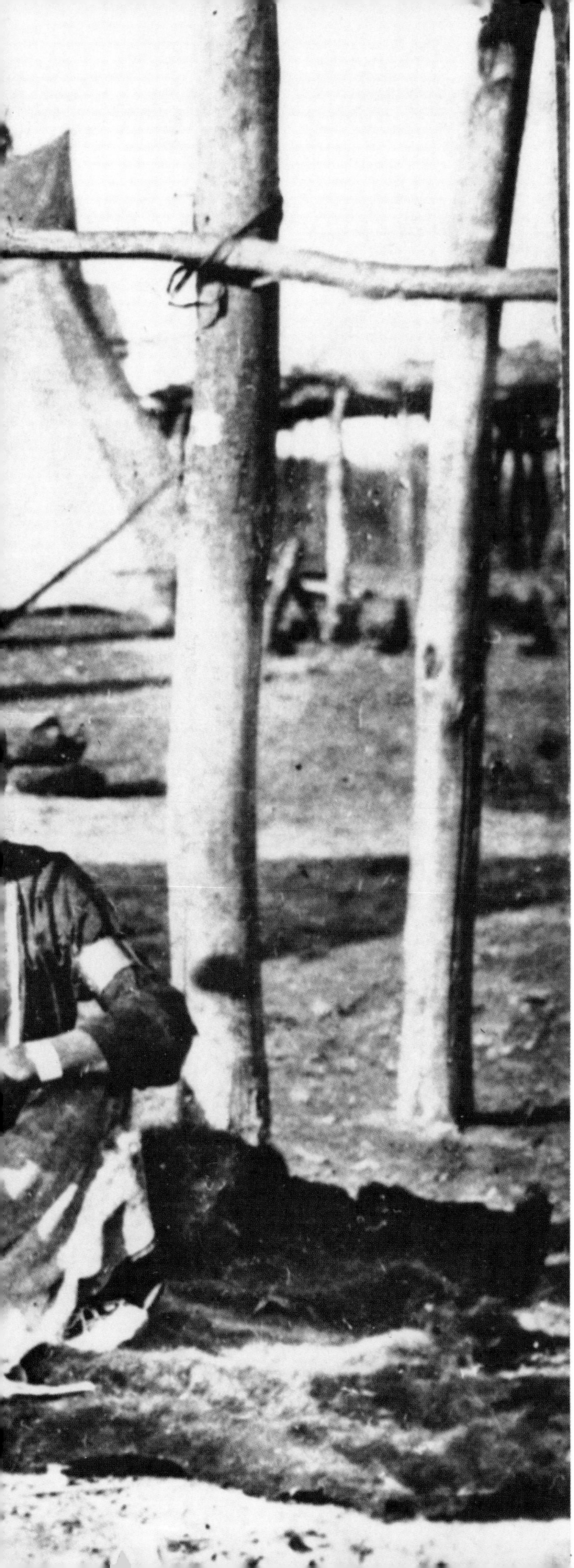

Pierre Garreau was photographed sitting in front of his earth lodge, and D. W. Longfellow was standing at his right at the Fort Berthold Indian Reservation in 1878. Lodges were constructed of log frames covered by brush, grass, and clay. The lodges were circular and measured twenty to forty feet in diameter. The ceiling had an opening for light which also served as a vent for smoke. Earth lodges were built so strong that people could sit on the roofs to look at the village and surrounding area. Courtesy of the SHSND

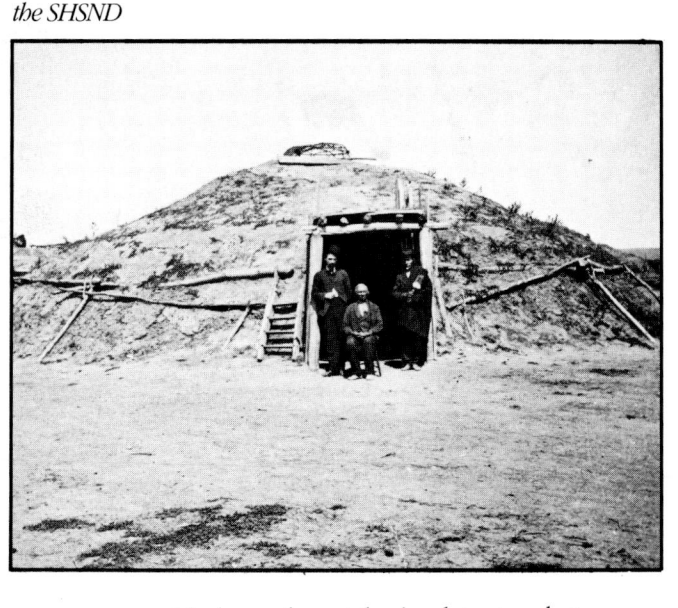

agreement with them, they staked a claim to what is now the northern third of North Dakota. The Chippewa adopted the tipi and a way of life centered on the bison. They lived in bands which acted independently from others. A tribal council and tribal police governed and maintained social order.

The Chippewa believed in the Great Spirit and a series of lesser spirits. The Mother Earth was the mother of mankind. Like other Plains Indians, the Chippewa believed the universe was the scene of an epic battle between spirits of good and evil. People had to please both good and evil spirits since these forces were present in themselves. The Chippewa danced a version of the Sun Dance and placed their dead on scaffolds or in trees.

The Cheyenne, Assiniboine, Crow, and Cree

Other groups of Indian peoples briefly inhabited or hunted in North Dakota during the last three hundred years. The Cheyenne, Assiniboine, Crow, and Cree were related to a number of the North Dakota tribes and competed and sometimes warred with them.

The Cheyenne people lived in central Minnesota before the 1700s. The Teton Sioux pushed the Cheyenne out of Minnesota as they moved west. The Cheyenne lived in southeastern North Dakota for a time, and during the 1700s migrated to the Missouri River Valley. The Mandan and Hidatsa drove them out, and by 1800 the Cheyenne relocated in the Black Hills at the headwaters of the Cheyenne River.

The Assiniboine were formerly part of the Yanktonai, but broke with that tribe in the early 1600s. They lived in the region between Lake Superior and Hudson Bay and by 1775 had migrated to the Saskatchewan and Assiniboine river valley. They hunted the plains of Canada and the northeastern part of North Dakota. The Assiniboine were closely allied with the Cree and often warred with the Teton Sioux over hunting grounds. Because of the ravages of smallpox epidemics, the Assiniboine joined with the Cree in the late 1830s. Though a woodland people in origin, the Assiniboine had adapted to a lifestyle on the plains and were as dependent on the bison as other Plains Indians.

The Crow people were once close to the Hidatsa, but during the late 1600s moved into the Yellowstone River Valley. The Crow adapted to life on the plains after leaving the Hidatsa. They occasionally hunted bison in North Dakota. The Cree people were allies of the Chippewa, but lived mostly in Canada. Some hunted in northeastern North Dakota, but never lived there.

The impact of Euro-American contact and subsequent domination of the native inhabitants

Red Buffalo Cow and Bad Gun were first and second chiefs of the Mandan people. Born in 1820, Bad Gun was a well-known warrior and was selected as chief of the Mandan in 1865. He was a representative of the Mandan people in Washington in 1875 and won important concessions for the tribe. Later, Bad Gun was in the Indian Police Service and judge of the Court of Indian Offenses Courtesy of the SHSND

Crazy Bull and Prairie Chicken were Hidatsa. The Hidatsa people were enemies of the Sioux and Chippewa, who forced them from northeastern North Dakota and northwestern Minnesota westward to the Missouri River around 1600. The Hidatsa were allies of the Mandan. By the time Lewis and Clark visited in 1804, the Hidatsa numbered around two thousand. Courtesy of the SHSND

f North Dakota are chronicled in following chapters of this book. However, the description of the lifestyles and people who are the native inhabitants of what is now North Dakota would not be complete without recounting some of the features of Indian life in modern North Dakota.

The past, present, and future of the American Indian was and will continue to be profoundly affected by United States government policy. The Indians of North Dakota are no exception to this axiom. From the 1850s to the 1870s, the United States government negotiated a series of treaties with North Dakota Indian tribes that guaranteed vast reservations where the Indians could live unmolested "as long as the grass grows." White settlers and the government never respected these treaties and through warfare, agreements, and fiat, the Indian reservations in North Dakota were reduced greatly in size by the end of the nineteenth century. Today there are four Indian reservations in North Dakota: the Fort Totten Reservation for the Dakota and Cut head Band of Yankton, established in 1867; the Fort Berthold Reservation for the Three Affiliated Tribes, established 1870; Standing Rock Reservation for the Dakota and Yanktonai, established 1867; and the Turtle Mountain Reservation for the Chippewa and Métis, established 1882. Part of a fifth, the Sisseton Reservation, lies largely in and is administered in South Dakota. Each reservation has an agency town where the tribal offices and government reside.

For a time, residence on the reservation was mandatory. While residing on the reservations, Indians were never far from supervision by the Indian agent appointed by the Bureau of Indian Affairs. Most whites thought Indians were brutal savages. Those interested in the welfare of Indians were paternalistic and committed to a course of action that would make Indians adopt white culture and reject their traditional lifestyles. According to Indian reformer Richard Henry Pratt, they sought to "kill the Indian and save the man." Indians on reservations were issued tools, plows, and food, and were expected to give up traditional lifestyles and become self-sufficient. During the 1870s, religious organizations were permitted to establish schools and welfare agencies on reservations. Catholics ran schools at Fort Totten, Standing Rock, and Turtle Mountain, and the Congregationalists had Fort Berthold. The Allotment Act or the Dawes Act of 1887 alloted reservation lands (which had been held communally by the tribes) to individuals on the reservations. The purpose of the Allotment Act was to give Indians a sense of ownership, sustenance, and force them to become agriculturalists. Indians who lived on alloted land could become U.S. citizens. The law allowed white settlement of the land that was left over after the allotment to Indians and later allowed Indians to sell the land to anyone. Many Indians sold or were tricked out of their land. By the end of the century, much of the reservations were in non-Indian hands. Today,

75 percent of the land on some North Dakota reservations is owned by non-Indians. Allotment was recognized as a mistake and abolished in 1934.

On the heels of the Allotment Act, a law creating a nationwide system of Indian boarding schools was enacted to educate Indian children. The purpose of the Indian boarding schools was to give young Indians a basic education, vocational or industrial skills, and indoctrination on western ways. The students were required to board at the school, many at a great distance from home, so young Indians would not continue to be corrupted by parents and their traditional way of life. Indian boarding schools in North Dakota were established in Bismarck, Wahpeton, and Fort Totten. By the end of the century, over 80 percent of all Indian students in the United States, nearly twenty-three thousand, attended one of the 113 government operated boarding schools.

During the 1920s, those who shaped U.S. government Indian policy began to have greater respect for Indian culture and a belief in cultural pluralism. Disillusionment over the failure of the boarding schools led to their closing during the 1930s and 1940s and replacement by local day schools and later public schools. Since those times, Indian education on the reservation has advanced slowly but dramatically, with creation of quality elementary, secondary, and higher education opportunities.

American Indians who were not citizens were extended U.S. citizenship in 1924. Reflecting the new attitude toward self-determination of Indian peoples, Congress enacted the Indian Reorganization Act (IRA) in 1934. The IRA created a system of self-government for Indian tribes on reservations. Tribal councils were given legitimacy and authority to govern and provide services to the people of the tribe. The IRA made funds available to try to buy back some of the land lost through allotment. Other funds were made available to provide educational, medical, agricultural, and social services for Indians. The idea of self-determination for Indians reached its zenith in 1975 with passage of the Indian Self-Determination and Education Assistance Act. The Act allows reservations to contract with the Bureau of Indian Affairs to administer their own services and schools. The only real shortcoming of the new policy is the lack of local funds sufficient to provide adequate support for services and schools.

Since 1900, the population of Native Americans in North Dakota has been increasing, from 6,969 to 20,157 in 1980. Many Indians today practice their native religions and live a traditional way of life. Social progress has been slow and difficult. Many Indians today are still dogged by poverty, poor education, unemployment and lack of opportunities, and a low standard of living. Despite these impediments, Native Americans, like all Americans, are striving to achieve self-respect, self-sufficiency, and unity.

Shown here are the wife of White Bear, Spotted Weasel and his wife, who were Hidatsa. Women were usually responsible for building the tipi or earth lodge, cooking or drying the meat, tanning animal skins for clothing, taking care of children, gardening, and gathering seeds and berries. Courtesy of the SHSND

This photograph of Many Bears and family, who were Arikara, is dated August 24, 1898. A complex of clan relationships comprised the social milieu the people lived in. Clan relationships often determined social position. The Arikara have clans in which the father determined membership. In Mandan and Hidatsa society, the mother determined membership. Courtesy of the SHSND

Mink Woman, a Hidatsa, was a granddaughter of Saka-kawea, Lewis and Clark's Shoshoni guide, and served as the model for the statue of Sakakawea standing on the state capital grounds. Courtesy of the SHSND

White Calf and family lived on the Fort Berthold Indian Reservation in August 1903. Courtesy of the SHSND

Young students attended the Congregational Mission School in Elbowoods, Fort Berthold Indian Reservation, June 1901. Government policy up to the 1880s assigned each reservation to a religious group to work with the Indians. In North Dakota, the Roman Catholics had Fort Totten and Standing Rock, and the Congregationalists had Fort Berthold. By 1890, twelve hundred Indian children attended the religious schools in North Dakota. Courtesy of the SHSND

The Rev. Charles L. Hall, head of the Congregational mission at the Fort Berthold Indian Reservation, posed with mission school students, Elbowoods, circa 1905. Charles Hall established the Congregational mission in 1876 and headed it until 1922. The Rev. Hall was succeeded by the Rev. Harold Case, who headed the mission until construction of Garrison Dam and subsequent flooding of Elbowoods and other reservation communities. Courtesy of the SHSND

The young women pictured here symbolize the change experienced by Native Americans in North Dakota over the last hundred years. They were photographed at the Fort Berthold Indian Reservation in 1972. Courtesy of the SHSND

Shown here is the White Shield School on the Fort Berthold Indian Reservation, in the 1950s. The emergence of new, modern, and local schools on Indian reservations did much to improve the quality of education for Native Americans. The advent of such institutions shows the federal government has recognized that the Indian boarding school system was largely a failure and that quality educational facilities on the reservation are a necessity. Courtesy of the SHSND

Indian School
Girls Orchestra
Bismarck, May 28-2

is the girls' orchestra from U.S. Indian School at Bismarck in 1925. Late in the last century, the federal government established a system of boarding schools to educate Indian children. The purpose of the Indian boarding schools was to give young Indians a basic education, vocational or industrial skills, and indoctrination in white ways. Students were required to board at the school, many at a great distance from home, so young Indians would not be disrupted by parents and their traditional way of life. Courtesy of the SHSND

Students of the U.S. Indian School at Bismarck are pictured in a classroom. A school for Sioux, Chippewa, and Blackfoot girls from tribes in the Dakotas and Montana, students received instruction in traditional academic subjects with special emphasis on home economics, music, and physical training. The school was opened in 1905 and closed in 1937. By then, federal Indian policy embodied the view that reservation schools were better than the boarding schools. Students of the Bismarck Indian School were transferred to reservation schools at Fort Yates and Fort Totten. Courtesy of the SHSND

...l Bodmer painted this ...kota warrior between ...33 and 1834. All the Indian ...es periodically raided ...ers to obtain food, horses, ...ves, and war honors. In ...st cases the raids were not ...ended to destroy the ...emy, but to punish or drive ...m from the area. Killing ...emies was generally viewed ...acceptable, but emphasis ...s placed on "counting ...up" by touching or striking ...ive enemy. The status of ...rriors depended to a large ...tent on their success in war-...re. Courtesy of the SHSND

A Sioux scaffold burial was photographed in 1882. The traditional Sioux belief is in a Great Spirit that is present in the earth, sky, moon, and rock; and in good and evil powers that struggle for mastery of the universe. The spirits of their dead travel to the Land of Many Lodges. Courtesy of the SHSND

...ton Sioux perform the Sun ...ance, circa 1832, in this ...inting by George Catlin. ...ancers had wooden pins ...aced through their shoulders ...ith buffalo skulls attached or ...ere suspended from poles by tethers attached to wooden pins inserted into their breasts. The Sun Dance was a means to ask the Great Spirit to provide a bountiful and meaningful life. Courtesy of the SHSND

These Sioux tipis near Fort Yates were located on the Standing Rock Indian Reservation. Indian women owned the tipi and were responsible for its manufacture and upkeep. Courtesy of the SHSND

Government distribution of oxen to the Sioux took place on the Standing Rock Indian Reservation, Fort Yates, circa 1910. Often by treaty arrangement, Indians received allotment of livestock, horses, farm equipment, and food to help sustain them. This policy often kept the Indians dependent on the federal government. Courtesy of the SHSND

These beautifully-painted Sioux Council tipis were located at Fort Yates. The tipi on the left is identified as One Bull's. The paintings on these sail duck canvas tipis are a rare example of northern plains pictographic art. Courtesy of the SHSND

Shown here is a contingent of the Fort Yates Indian Police, Standing Rock Indian Reservation. Under the supervision of the Indian Agent, the Indian Police maintained order and peace on the reservation. The Indian Police were involved in the arrest and shooting death of Sitting Bull during the Ghost Dance Movement in 1890. Courtesy of the SHSND

In 1876, Benedictine Abbot Martin Marty established a Catholic mission at Fort Yates. Pictured here are Fr. Bernard Strassmeier, seated right, Fr. Ambrose, seated left, and possibly Fr. Martin Kenel, standing on the left. The other priests and Indians are not identified. This photo probably dates from 1910. Courtesy of the SHSND

Students pose in front of the Fort Yates Indian boarding school. In addition to English instruction and basic academic subjects, boys at Indian boarding schools were provided manual and industrial training, girls were trained in the domestic arts, and all were taught citizenship and Christianity. Courtesy of the SHSND

Gall (1839-1894) was one of the Sioux chiefs involved in the Battle of the Little Big Horn. After the battle, Gall helped lead some of the Sioux people from their Canadian refuge and accepted reservation status in the United States. Gall was an important Sioux leader at the Standing Rock Indian Reservation. Courtesy of the SHSND

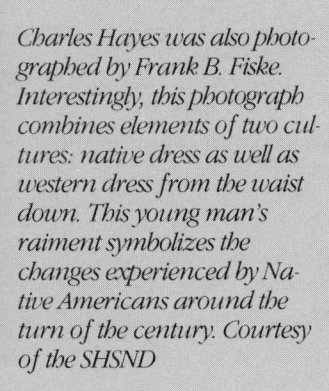

Charles Hayes was also photographed by Frank B. Fiske. Interestingly, this photograph combines elements of two cultures: native dress as well as western dress from the waist down. This young man's raiment symbolizes the changes experienced by Native Americans around the turn of the century. Courtesy of the SHSND

The John Gayton family was photographed by the noted Indian portraitist Frank B. Fiske, Fort Yates. Frank Fiske was born in 1883 at Fort Bennett in South Dakota. His family moved to Fort Yates in 1889. The young Fiske aspired to be a steamboat pilot, but as an adult pursued his other passion—photography. Operating the photo studio at Fort Yates, Fiske concentrated on making portrait studies of the Indian men, women, and children of the Standing Rock Indian Reservation, as well as studying the culture and history of the Sioux people. Fiske's camera also documented many events and places throughout central North Dakota. Many of his photographs appear in this chapter and in other chapters as well. Courtesy of the SHSND

A-na-shi-u, (Chippewa), was a member of the Turtle Mountain Reservation Indian Police. Reservation life for the Chippewa was very difficult for many years. The government seized 90 percent of their land and later paid them about ten cents an acre. Little of the reservation was good for farming, and with the buffalo gone, many starved. Courtesy of the SHSND

The wedding of Harry Graybear and Maggie Standing Soldier occurred at Fort Yates on July 30, 1916. Federal Indian policy in the nineteenth and early twentieth centuries was to civilize and Christianize the Indians. Indians were expected to give up their language and traditional way of life. Courtesy of the SHSND

John Spear and William Bouga posed for this photo on the Fort Totten Indian Reservation, circa 1900. The Allotment Act of 1887 distributed land on the reservations to families and individuals, with the land left over open to non-Indians for settlement. The purpose of the Allotment Act was to give Indians a sense of private ownership, sustenance, and to force them to become agriculturalists. Courtesy of the SHSND

A Chippewa woman works on a wooden bowl. Indians are skilled at making a wide variety of tools from natural raw materials. Stone, wood, bone, sinew, antlers, leather, and clay were widely used by the Indians. Courtesy of the SHSND

These Chippewa Sun Dancers lived on the Turtle Mountain Indian Reservation. The Chippewa danced a Sun Dance similar to the Sioux dance. Accompanied by singing and prayers, the dance lasted four days and three nights. The shoulders of Sun Dancers were pierced and thongs were passed through and attached to a tall pole. Dancers were accompanied by special songs. The ritual concluded with a feast. Courtesy of the SHSND

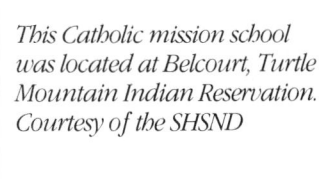

This Catholic mission school was located at Belcourt, Turtle Mountain Indian Reservation. Courtesy of the SHSND

The Chippewa were divided into clans named after animals, birds, or fish. The clan was the most important group to the Chippewa. Clan membership was inherited and passed on through the father; marriage between two people belonging to the same clan was forbidden. Courtesy of the SHSND

Gingras Trading Post near Walhalla, established in the 1840s, is one of the few remains of the Red River Valley fur trade. Métis trader Antoine B. Gingras at one time owned a chain of trading posts across northern Dakota and southern Manitoba. The buildings are a state historic site administered by the State Historical Society of North Dakota. Courtesy of the SHSND

3

THE FRONTIER 1738-1890

In the early eighteenth century the English colonies clung precariously to the Atlantic coast, with nearly all settlement within one hundred miles of the ocean. In addition to these colonies, the English Hudson's Bay Company territory lay north of New France, the French Territory primarily populated along the Saint Lawrence River but stretching east to west from the Alleghenies to the Rockies and north to south from above the Great Lakes to the Gulf of Mexico. To the south was Spanish Territory in present-day New Mexico, Texas, and Florida. Present-day North Dakota lay in an area claimed by both England and France. In 1762, during the French and Indian War, the territory between the Mississippi River and the Rocky Mountains (with the exception of the region drained by the Red and Souris rivers) came under Spain's rule, while the treaty which ended that war in 1763 placed the remainder of what had been New France under English control. Louisiana Territory was again acquired for France in 1800 by Napoleon Bonaparte, who in turn sold it to the United States in 1803.

To the Europeans and to the Euro-Americans who were to follow, the western frontier was an area to explore and to exploit. Exploration was undertaken to establish claims to these territories, to search for a water route to the west, to gain scientific information, and to search for new sources of furs. As with much of the western frontier, the fur trade brought the first white peoples to the area of North Dakota. The fur traders were followed by other explorers, surveyors, the military, and, eventually, the settlers from whom most present-day residents are descended.

The first of these explorers was Pierre Gaultier de Varennes, the Sieur de La Verendrye (1685-1749), who had established a string of small forts stretching westward from Lake Superior, thereby staking New France's claim to the western country and at the same time challenging the English fur traders at Hudson Bay. In 1738 La Verendrye and his sons set out from their post on the Assiniboine River and entered what is now North Dakota. While their visit with the Mandan lasted only a short time, it was the first recorded contact between whites and Indians in the Dakotas.

Several foreign powers vied for control of the Northern Plains fur trade. The first to dominate the trade were the French. With the defeat of the French in the French and Indian War in 1763 the British took control. Working from the north out of Hudson Bay and Montreal, Hudson's Bay

Shown here is Meriwether Lewis. The expedition of Lewis and William Clark from 1804 to 1806 inspired American interest in the Upper Missouri region. Courtesy of the SHSND

Fort Manuel Lisa is shown as it appeared in 1812. Manuel Lisa entered the fur trade in Saint Louis. Inspired by the reports of Lewis and Clark, Lisa and his party set off in 1807 for the Upper Missouri. His success led to the establishment of the Missouri Fur Company and the building of trading forts on the Missouri River, including Fort Manuel Lisa twelve miles north of the Knife River in 1809-10. Lisa's boats were reported to have brought out $35,000 worth of furs in one season. Courtesy of the SHSND

Company and North West Company traders established themselves among the Mandan and other Upper Missouri Indians. Several posts were built by the British along the Red River Valley, which later developed into the first settlements in northeastern North Dakota. The first settlement in present-day North Dakota was founded when the North West Company built a post on the Pembina River in 1797. Named after the Chippewa term for a common cranberry bush, Pembina became a fur trade center along the Red River. Company rivalries, boundary disputes, and smuggling activities were common in this border town.

The Spanish tried but failed to dislodge the British from the newly acquired Louisiana Territory. When Americans later acquired that territory they also had trouble ousting the British because of the long distance and the Indian hostilities encountered between Saint Louis and the Upper Missouri. After the War of 1812 and the development of steamboat traffic on the Missouri, American fur traders under John Jacob Astor's American Fur Company dominated the trade.

Lewis and Clark's celebrated journey to the Pacific from 1804 to 1806 marked the first of many government-sponsored operations on the Northern Plains. These early military efforts centered on establishing United States sovereignty in the lands recently acquired by the Louisiana Purchase. After initially defining British/United States boundaries, military expeditions concentrated on surveying, mapping, and exploring other parts of the territory. The information thus gleaned enabled westward expansion to take place.

One of the primary goals of the Lewis and Clark mission had been to determine the suitability of the Trans-Missouri West for the fur trade. The information gathered on the region's fur-bearing animals, the native inhabitants' attitudes to the fur trade, and the waterways that could serve as transportation networks were crucial to opening the Northern Plains fur trade to the Americans, a fur trade actively engaged in by British traders at the time Lewis and Clark came through North Dakota.

Shortly after Lewis and Clark's journey, American traders traveled up the Missouri to the Rocky Mountain region where they hoped to establish trading posts. That region was particularly rich in beavers and other fur bearers in demand by fashion-conscious Europeans. Their early attempts failed, largely because of transportation problems and hostilities from the Blackfeet who would not trade with Americans nor allow hunting in their territory.

As a result, fur trading efforts concentrated on the northern Great Plains, which was relatively accessible from Saint Louis and whose native inhabitants were willing to trade. Although Alexander Henry established one of the first trading posts in North Dakota when he built North West Company's Park River Post near Pembina in 1800, it wasn't until Saint Louis businessman Manuel Lisa formed the Missouri Fur Company that American trading posts were established on the Upper Missouri. Fort Manuel Lisa, built near the mouth of the Knife River in 1809, provided a base for trapping in Montana's rich beaver country. The War of 1812 interrupted Lisa's success.

By the mid-nineteenth century, American fur trade companies had established several posts along the Missouri and succeeded in dislodging British fur traders from the area. Established in 1829 near the Missouri-Yellowstone confluence, Fort Union was a major post for the American Fur Company. It served as a trading center for furs produced in Crow and Blackfoot lands to the west, and for Assiniboine and Plains Cree hunters.

Forts were not only trading centers, but also depots for supplies and furs, defensible residential quarters, agricultural and manufacturing centers and social centers where ideas and customs were exchanged between Indians and traders. Fort locations were chosen largely for their accessibility to Indian groups. A good wood supply for fuel and building supplies, as well as proximity to major rivers for transporting goods to and from Saint Louis were also important factors in choosing a site.

Diminishing beaver populations and the introduction of silk top hats marked the decline of the beaver fur trade and placed a new emphasis on the buffalo robe trade. Buffalo numbers were still high and the skins were in demand for use as lap robes and other winter garments. In addition, steamboat navigation on the Missouri made transport of the heavy and bulky robes affordable.

The fur trade era brought two cultures together, made the region politically and economically important, and paved the way for regional settlement. In addition, a new ethnic group emerged as a result of the fur trade—the Métis (derived from the French word for "mixed"). Born of French, Scottish, or English fur traders and Cree,

Born in New Orleans in 1772, Manuel Lisa undertook the first large-scale American effort to begin trading in the Upper Missouri region in 1807. Described as hardy, bold and daring, Lisa came to be trusted by the Indians with whom he traded. He continued to travel the Missouri region until his death in 1820. Courtesy of the SHSND

Built in 1828, Fort Union was the most important of the American Fur Company's (or Upper Missouri Outfit) twenty-three forts in the northwest. Situated at the confluence of the Yellowstone and Missouri rivers, Fort Union served as a trading post until 1866. The site of Fort Union is now administered by the National Park Service. Courtesy of the SHSND

Henry Boller was a young Pennsylvanian who worked for the "opposition" to the Upper Missouri Outfit (American Fur Company). Boller began his fur-trading experience at Fort Atkinson between 1858 and 60, where Frost, Todd and Company competed with the Upper Missouri Outfit post, Fort Berthold. Boller would write a book about his experiences "in the Far West." Courtesy of the SHSND

Francis Chardon built Fort Berthold in 1845 near the Hidatsa settlement of Like-a-Fishhook Village, named for the bend in the river. The Mandans moved to the village a few years later and the Arikaras joined them in 1862. Courtesy of the SHSND

Ojibwa, or Assiniboine mothers, the Métis identified with neither the whites nor the Indians. They blended elements of both cultures to form their own society, and based their economy on buffalo hunts and the fur trade. Although they hunted on the western plains, Métis settlements were established along the Red River Valley in North Dakota and Canada, many of which exist today. While their dual heritage gave the Métis access to both Native and European worlds, they were often denied political recognition. On two occasions (1869-1879; 1885), Louis Riel led resistance movements against the Canadian government over Métis land rights and political representation. Each time Riel set up a provisional government. Although the Canadian government met some of the demands, many Métis fled to western Canada and North Dakota. In the end, Riel was found guilty of treason and hanged.

As the nineteenth century progressed, the former English colonies no longer clung to the Atlantic coast as they had a century before. As the Americans moved west, the Upper Great Plains began to be viewed differently. Until the 1850s, relatively peaceful relations prevailed between Indians and Euro-Americans on the Northern Plains. The fur trade dominated these early contacts and brought marked benefits to both parties, yet it also planted the seeds of future conflict. Epidemics of measles, influenza, and smallpox—European diseases to which Indians had no natural immunity—spread among Indian tribes. The 1837 smallpox epidemic is linked with the arrival at Fort Clark of the American Fur Company's supply steamboat, *Saint Peters.* Smallpox soon claimed 90 percent of the Mandan population. Disease, alcoholism, competition between foreign powers, and finally, the discovery of gold and the desire for new lands led to growing tensions. As a result, the U.S. government intervened, first through peace commissions and

treaties, later through military campaigns.

One example of this change and growing conflict was the Euro-American view of the buffalo. The buffalo herds of the Plains played a key role in frontier life in Dakota Territory. Both the Indian and the Euro-American were dependent on them. For the Indians, the buffalo provided food, shelter, and even transportation (in the form of bull boats). To the fur trader, the buffalo was a source of food, but more importantly it represented a fur commodity to be sold in foreign and eastern markets.

Later Euro-Americans held more negative views of the buffalo. To the immigrants the herds were obstacles to westward settlement; the U.S. military saw opportunities to control the Indians by controlling the availability of the herds. As a result, professional hunters were allowed to kill the herds under the protection of the U.S. Army. In the end, the herds which had occupied the plains for centuries narrowly escaped extinction. The 1870s and 1880s marked the end of the seemingly limitless herds.

Completion of the transcontinental Union Pacific Railroad in the late 1860s divided the Great Plains into two vast buffalo ranges, resulting in a northern herd and a southern herd. The general slaughter of the southern herd occurred between 1870 and 1876. The destruction of the northern herd came later, with most of the killing taking place from 1880 to 1883.

The Great Plains and particularly the upper Great Plains were, for a time, an obstacle to cross. This was especially true with the discovery of gold in California, Nevada, and the Rocky Mountains, By the 1850s and 1860s military efforts shifted away from exploration and toward peace-keeping. Peace commissions and military forts were established. The former provided negotiators for the Indian treaties, while the latter provided military forces to protect immigrants and accompanying

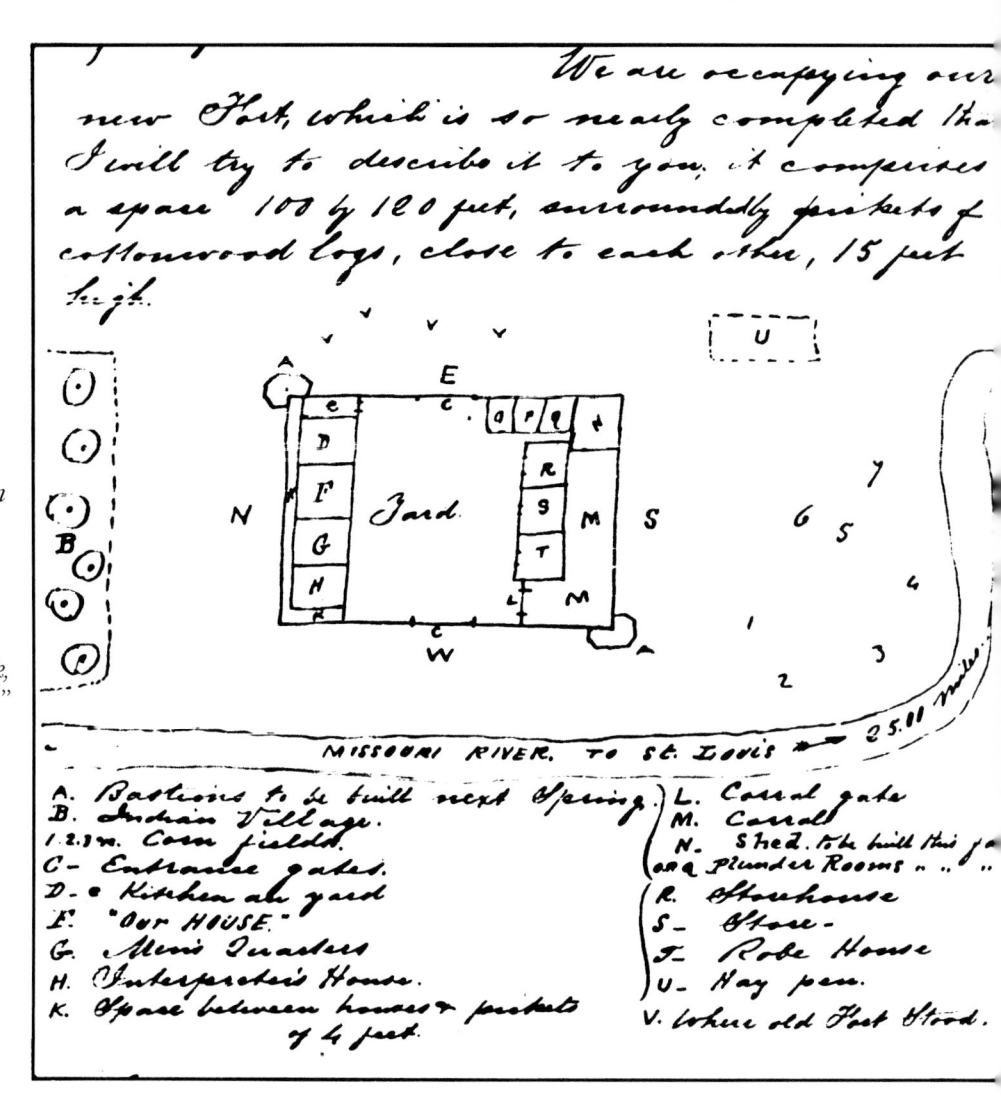

Boller described Fort Atkinson to his father in a letter home in 1858. "Our force," he wrote, "consists of the Bourgeoise [commander of the post], myself, six men, one courier or Express Rider, cook, and two or three interpreters." Courtesy of the SHSND

infrastructure such as railroad survey and construction crews. United States policy in the early nineteenth century had been to establish large Indian "concentrations" which impeded the settlers' movement across the plains. In the 1850s the government initiated a new policy of establishing "reservations," small units that would make it easier for settlers to move. In 1851, the government negotiated a treaty with the Sioux, the Blackfeet, the Mandan, the Crow, and other tribes at Fort Laramie. As a result of this treaty, each of these groups was to withdraw to smaller reservations.

Fort Abercrombie was the first military post established in present-day North Dakota. Established on the Red River in 1857, the post was briefly abandoned and rebuilt in 1860. Fort Abercrombie served as the starting point for navigation down the Red River (the *Anson Northrop*, the first steamboat on the Red River, started from here in 1859), and for the first of the wagon trains to the Montana gold fields (eight expeditions traveled through northern Dakota between 1862 and 1867).

Growing tensions over dwindling reservation lands, failures to meet treaty provisions, and near starvation conditions led to a major Indian attack against Minnesota settlers and ultimately to military campaigns against Indians in northern Dakota. During the Minnesota Uprising of 1862

Fort Abercrombie came under siege for nearly three weeks until a force from Saint Paul provided relief.

Although the Minnesota militia under the command of Henry Hastings Sibley, a trader for the American Fur Company and a colonel in the militia, had defeated the Sioux, the Army determined to undertake a major expedition to puni them. A two-pronged attacked was planned against the Sioux with one military column und Sibley, now commissioned a brigadier general volunteers, marching toward Devils Lake from Minnesota. The other column, under Gen. Alfre Sully, would follow the Missouri River into northern Dakota and then turn toward Devils Lake. The Sioux would be caught between the two columns. Because Sully's column was late arriving in northern Dakota, the plan did not work. Both armies engaged the Sioux in battle—Sibley at Big Mound, Dead Buffalo Lake, and Stony Lake, and Sully at Whitestone Hill, the bloodiest battle ever fought on North Dakota so In effect, the "Minnesota Massacre" had been countered by a northern Dakota massacre, but few of the Sioux engaged in battle with Sibley and Sully had taken any part in the uprising in Minnesota.

The discovery of gold in California and Montana brought increased travel through Indi lands via river and overland routes. Because thi affic went through traditional hunting grounds and threatened their way of life, many Indian tribes protested westward expansion. Frequent attacks against miners and settlers resulted in government intervention. The Fort Laramie Treaty of 1851 had been an initial attempt to define land boundaries for several Plains Indian tribes, but continued hostilities and misunderstandings required subsequent treaties. In 1868, another Fort Laramie treaty was signed. It defined reserva- tion boundaries and guaranteed Indian rights to hunt outside the reservation. It also forbade Euro-American encroachment on Indian lands and called for the abandonment of the much-hated Bozeman trail. Whites violating these and other treaties culminated in the Indian Wars.

Fort Abercrombie was the first military post in present-day North Dakota. Starting with the con- struction of Fort Rice in 1864, however, a series of permanent posts were built on the Missouri River. By 1867, Fort Buford and Fort Stevenson had been built further up the Missouri. Two addi- tional forts were constructed in 1867, Fort Totten near Devils Lake and Fort Ransom on the Cheyenne River. In the 1870s the list also included Forts Pembina, Abraham Lincoln, Seward, and Yates.

The Army posts dotting the map of Dakota Territory served several purposes. They provided bases for military expeditions, offered escort

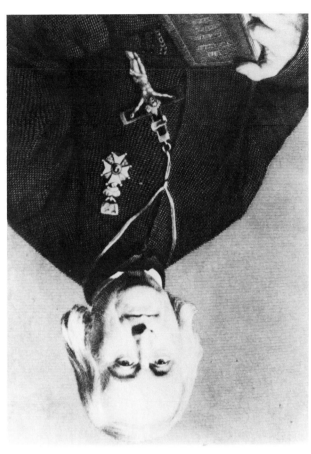

Father Pierre Jean DeSmet was one of the most famous missionaries to spend time in the region. Father DeSmet, a Jesuit, stopped to preach to traders and Indians in northern Dakota during voyages in the area between 1839 and 1868. Father DeSmet was never harmed in his visits to the Upper Missouri area. Other missionaries were not as fortunate. Baptist Elijah Terry was killed by the Sioux in 1852; the wife of Congre- gational missionary David Spencer was killed in 1855. Missionaries faced severe hardships for themselves and their families to carry the Gospel to the traders and Indians residing in northern Dakota. Courtesy of the SHSND

Norman Kitson's post is depicted at Pembina in the 1840s. Trading posts had been located at Pembina from 1797, when C. J. B. Chaboillez established a post there. After the Red River flooded in 1851, Kitson decided to move his headquarters to St. Joseph (Walhalla). Courtesy of the SHSND

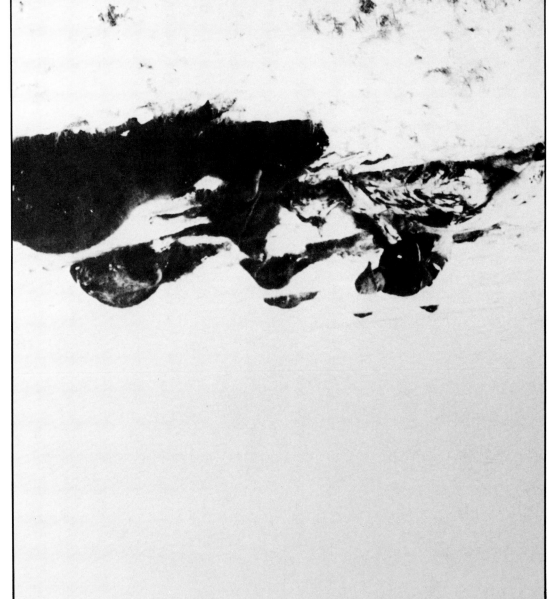

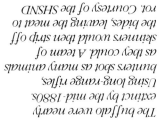

The Métis hauled furs to St. Paul in high-wheeled Red River carts, shown here near the Canadian border. The squeaking from the unlubri-cated wooden wheels could be heard long distances. Courtesy of the SHSND

The buffalo were nearly extinct by the mid-1880s. Using long-range rifles, hunters shot as many animals as they could. A team of skinners would then strip off the hides, leaving the meat to rot. Courtesy of the SHSND

protection, and later policed nearby Indian agencies. Forts were built at strategic locations throughout the territory, each successive post signaling an advance in the military frontier. By the mid-1880s most were no longer needed and the forts were gradually abandoned—Fort Seward in 1877, Forts Abercrombie and Rice in 1878, Fort Stevenson in 1883, Fort Totten in 1890, Fort Abraham Lincoln in 1891, Forts Buford and Pembina in 1895, and Fort Yates in 1903.

Army life varied over the period of time the frontier posts existed. The earliest soldiers faced the greatest hardships, building and living in hastily-constructed quarters far from civilization. Over time, new post buildings generally offered better accommodations and life became somewhat easier as the areas became more settled. Soldiers at Fort Totten who ventured out of the post carrying the mail on the Totten Trail encountered real danger, while post life provided mostly boredom. Soldiers at Fort Buford from 1866 to 1867 saw plenty of action, and military expeditions away from the relative safety of the military post generally meant hard and dangerous duty. The troops, about half of whom were foreigners, occasionally suffered under incompetent and drunken commanders, such as the first post commander at Fort Totten, Capt. Samuel A. Wainwright. Often alcoholism and disease were far greater menaces to the frontier soldier than

were the Sioux.

Gen. George Custer's expedition in 1874 confirmed the discovery of gold in the Black Hills and prompted an invasion of that area by gold-seekers. Efforts to turn back the gold-seekers from this area guaranteed to the Indians by the Treaty of 1868 sparked the Sioux War of 1876. The federal government had ordered all Indians onto reservations late in 1875, but the Army set off in the spring of 1876 to deal with the Indians who ignored the edict. It was in this well-known campaign that Custer and more than two hundred soldiers were killed. The news shocked the nation and sealed the fate of the Sioux. Military reinforcements poured in and doggedly pursued the Indians until the Sioux finally gave in and sold the Black Hills. Sitting Bull and a small remnant of followers held out until 1881, finally surrendering at Fort Buford. Sitting Bull, who took pride in never having signed a treaty with the whites, was killed in 1890 while being arrested during the controversy over the Ghost Dance. Two weeks later Big Foot and three hundred of his band were killed by the Seventh Cavalry at Wounded Knee Creek in South Dakota. The tragedy at Wounded Knee marked the end of an era in which the Indians had continually resisted white encroachment. From this point on, the Indians would be restricted to a sedentary existence on reservations.

The United States census of 1850 reported 1,116 persons at Pembina, the occupation of most of the men listed as "hunter." The large, annual hunts by Métis from both sides of the border greatly reduced the buffalo herds. The Canadian hunters' incursion drew protests from the Chippewas, Sioux, American traders, and the United States government. Courtesy of the SHSND

These buffalo hides were ready for shipment from Dickinson in 1883. The skinners staked the hides out on the cold ground. Later, when they were stiff, the hides were piled as shown and buyers offered a price for them. One observer recalled seeing a trainload of buffalo hides leave Bismarck in 1876, and reported that one firm in Montana shipped sixty-thousand buffalo hides that same year. Courtesy of the SHSND

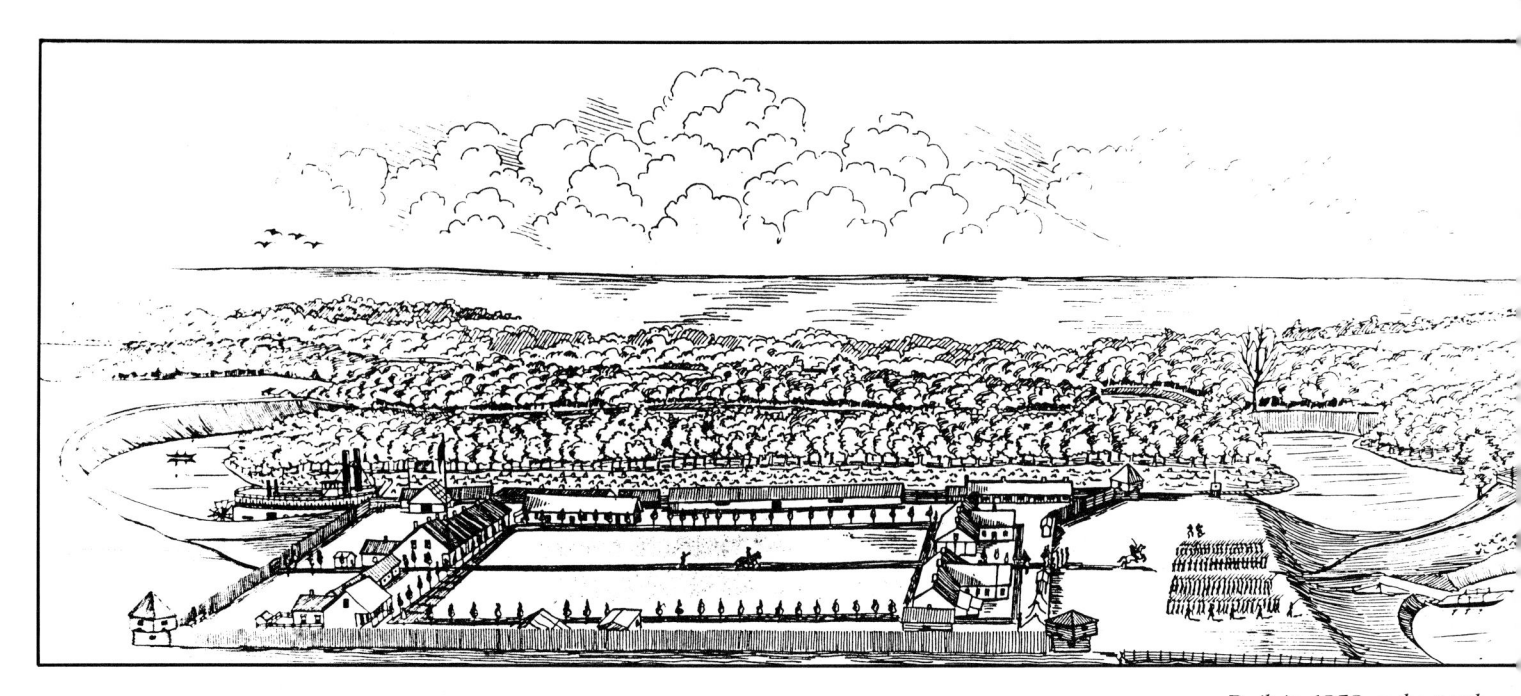

Built in 1858 as the north-eastern anchor of the northern plains military frontier, Fort Abercrombie became the jumping off point for wagon trains heading for the gold fields of Montana and the head of navigation on the Red River. Abandoned in 1878, the post's location is now administered as a state historic site. Courtesy of the SHSND

General Sully used artillery
llery at the Killdeer Moun-
in Battle in 1864. Courtesy
the SHSND

lthough delayed in bringing
's army up the Missouri
uring the 1863 campaign,
en. Alfred Sully did engage
battle, attacking an Indian
llage at Whitestone Hill. The
efeat was inflicted on the
anktonai Sioux, however,
ther than the Santees Sully
as supposedly pursuing.
ourtesy of the SHSND

As a result of the campaign of 1863, Gen. Alfred Sully established Fort Rice (shown here as it appeared in 1868), near the Cannonball River in the summer of 1864. Courtesy of the SHSND

The Sully expedition camped near Fort Berthold in 1864. Courtesy of the SHSND

The first newspaper in what is now North Dakota was published by soldiers stationed at Fort Union in 1864. When the publishers were transferred to Fort Rice, the paper moved as well, continuing until 1865. Courtesy of the SHSND

FRONTIER SCOUT

Winegar & Goodwin, Publishers.   LIBERTY AND UNION.   Co. I 30th Wis. Vols., Proprietors.

Vol. 1.   FORT UNION, D. T., AUGUST 17, 1864.   No. 4.

—The steamer Gen. Grant arrived at our levee last Saturday evening from Fort Rice. She returned down the river after discharging a large pile of government freight.

—A soldier by the name of Jerome Mc-Carty, belonging to Co. "L" 7th Iowa Cavalry, was drowned at this place last evening, while attempting to swim his horse across the river. He is reported as being a good swimmer and it is supposed that he was injured by his horse.

—Blessed are they who remember the printers, and PATRICK & HULL, of the Fort Union bakery, are among the number. They presented us, a few days since, with some of those nice pies which they are baking every day. They inform us that they are now prepared to bake for any who may desire to furnish their own materials.

—The following complimentary notices from some of our friends will speak for themselves;

FORT RICE, July 6th, 1864.

PUBLISHERS OF THE SCOUT:—Inclosed please find five dollars to be placed to my credit on the books of the FRONTIER SCOUT. This little, clean, and fresh sheet from the northern boundary of the United States entitles you to great credit, and we appreciate the difficulties you are obliged to overcome in issuing it.

Hoping that your paper will continue successful, and that Co. I will return to Wisconsin with its 101 aggregate to muster out,   I remain yours, &c.,
    T. C. S.

The following extract is taken from a private letter:

"The FRONTIER SCOUT, that neat, cheerful, little sheet comes greeting us ever like a sunbeam of intelligence representing civilization and enlightenment and reminding me of a beautiful flower blooming alone in a desert land receiving its nourishment, like a fairy, from the passing breeze. May long live the SCOUT. Success, future prosperity and fame to Messrs. Winegar & Goodwin, Publishers. Health, happiness and long life to the Proprietors.

"We have received the first number of the FRONTIER SCOUT, published at Fort Union, Dakota Territory, by Winegar & Goodwin, Co. "I," 30th Wis. Vols. proprietors. It is a good deal of a paper, and gotten up regardless of expense."

[Sioux City Register]

—The want of room obliges us to omit several articles of importance this week.

B. B's.—Do you not know what B. B. means? Well, we'll tell you. It means bed bugs! Yes, bed bugs! We have heard of bed bugs very often by people who had seen them; we have heard travelers mention the fact that they have been obliged to set up in bed with a candle in one hand and a revolver in the other in order to retain possession of their beds; we have heard yarns told about them until we thought man's imagination could go no farther in creating stories, for we always considered them as gotten up for the purpose of killing time. But "a change came o'er the spirit of my dream," and we are satisfied that the half has not been told. We have seen them—seen them in battalions—seen them in divisions and in army corps, and they were of all sizes from the smallest, four of which can stand on the head of a pin, up to the size of a mud turtle. We have seen them regularly organized—thoroughly drilled—and apparently in a good state of discipline; at first they would throw out a few foragers who would wait very quietly until we were asleep when they would draw what blood they could carry and go quietly off. For the sake of maintaining peace we submitted until they came in force one night and attempted to carry us off bodily; then we objected as an American citizen bound to maintain our rights. But it was of no use, we were obliged to leave and seek repose elsewhere; we finally took refuge in the farther corner of the room on the floor; there we thought they would not find us, and for one night they left us in peace, but before the next night their skirmishers had ascertained our exact locality, and before we were fairly asleep they came at us in full force, but we were determined to maintain our position or perish in the attempt. Charge after charge they made which we successfully repulsed with a trifling loss of blood on our side. At length they changed their tactics, and one much larger than the others advanced to the attack alone; then came the tug of war, and for a long time neither side could claim any advantage; we were rapidly losing strength and thought our time had come —we remembered that our life was not

insured, and all the actions of it seemed to pass in rapid succession before us; we thought upon our home and those dear ones that were anxiously waiting our return, and we determined to struggle to the bitter end; at length fortune favored us and by a brilliant manoeuver we were enabled to place our opponent on his back and plunging a knife into him finished him. The rest were apparently thunder struck and stood unable to do anything but gaze, so taking advantage of their surprise we seized our blankets and once more fled. That stands as the one eventful night of a life time—never shall we forget the horrors of it.

Our next resort was to the porch thinking they would let us have at least one side of the house—the outside; but after one or two nights they were after us again, although not in so great numbers yet sufficiently strong to keep us constantly on the alert. We soon found out that we could not stay there long so we looked round for new quarters where we might be secure at least for a few nights until we should somewhat recover; we at length hit upon the observatory on top of the house; waiting until darkness had settled upon the face of the earth we again seized our blankets and like a thief we stole very quietly up through the attic and out on to the observatory when we lay down and had a good night's rest. Three days have passed and they have not found our last retreat yet but expect every day they will; so we are prepared to flee again; this time we shall take refuge on top of the flag staff, and roost after the manner of a bird; after attaining our elevated position we shall hire a cheap boy to sweep the bottom of the flag staff continually so they will be unable to reach us. We are now quite reduced in flesh and any one can see that we have not another drop of blood to spare.

B. B's have become a perfect terror to us; sleeping or waking they are continually in our mind; our dreams are filled with monster bed bugs and during our waking moments they are ever present—do we sit down to write they are crawling over the paper by dozens—do we sit down to play a social game of cards bed bugs form the hearts, diamonds, spades, and clubs. We talk of nothing but bed bugs; the other day a man asked us the time of day we replied "bed bugs," and so it goes. Bed bugs have become the bane of our life and we fear that we shall go crazy soon unless there is something done.

Units of black soldiers, term
"buffalo soldiers," served c
the frontier. Carter Huse u
an infantryman with the
Twenty-fifth Infantry stationed at Fort Buford. Anc
black unit, the Tenth Cava
also served at Fort Buford.
Courtesy of the SHSND

Fort Buford was built near
Fort Union at the strategically
important confluence of the
Missouri and Yellowstone
rivers. The site had been sur-
veyed by General Sully in
1864. This early photo shows
the stockade, blockhouse, and
barracks in the right of the
picture. Courtesy of the
SHSND

Winter at Fort Stevenson
(established 1867) is depicted
in a painting by Gen. Philippe
Régis de Trobriand, the fort's
commander. The mud chink-
ing between the logs shrank
when it froze, leaving cracks
through which snow sifted
onto the floor and formed
drifts. Courtesy of the SHSND

63

Fort Abraham Lincoln is shown as it appeared in 1873, the year it was completed and combined with the infantry post on the hill next to it, Fort McKeen. In 1876 many of the soldiers stationed here would lose their lives at the Little Big Horn. In the far right of the picture is officers row with the commanding officer's quarters in the middle of the row of houses. Courtesy of the SHSND

Camp Hancock was established at Bismarck prior to the coming of the Northern Pacific Railroad. The military then moved to Fort McKeen and Fort Abraham Lincoln across the Missouri River. Courtesy of the SHSND

Fort Totten, on Devils Lake, is shown as it appeared shortly after it was established in 1867. The soldiers' isolation in this period is evident. Many soldiers would be enticed to stay, however, taking up homesteads or helping to settle nearby towns. Courtesy of the SHSND

The commanding officer's quarters at Fort Abraham Lincoln, was sometimes referred to as "Custer's house." When the original house burned, General Custer had a larger, more commodious house built. Courtesy of the SHSND

In 1874, Gen. George A. Custer led an expedition from Fort Abraham Lincoln to the Black Hills, confirming the presence of gold. Courtesy of the SHSND

The Custers enterained guests in their parlor at Fort Abraham Lincoln. Elizabeth Custer probably received the news here of her husband's death, which was brought to her by Capt. Stephen A. Baker, of the Sixth Infantry, and Bismarck Mayor John A. McLean. Not long after the post was abandoned, local residents dismantled the house and the other post buildings and carted them away. Courtesy of the SHSND

The confirmation of gold set off a rush for the Black Hills—land guaranteed by treaty to the Sioux—setting up a sequence of events that would culminate in the war in 1876. Courtesy of the SHSND

The Far West, *piloted by Capt. Grant Marsh, brought the wounded and the bad news back from the Little Big Horn, a trip of 920 miles which was completed in only fifty-four hours. Built at Pittsburgh, Pennsylvania, in 1870, the 397 ton stern-wheeler was 190 feet long and thirty-three feet wide. Consistently profitable, it was considered a lucky boat, operating without a serious accident, until*

October 30, 1883, when it was sunk by a snag at Mullanthy Island, below Saint Charles, Missouri.

Suspended upright, near the bow of the boat, are the spars. Dropped at the appropriate angle, the heavy poles were used to push the boat back or sideways when navigating off sandbars on the shallow upper Missouri. Courtesy of the SHSND

Soldiers posed around the water wagon at Fort Steve son in 1867. Much of a soldier's time was consum in such routine tasks as th Courtesy of the SHSND

...own here is a cabin on the ...eamboat Far West. *Courtesy ...f the SHSND*

In the foreground of the artillery battery is a Gatling gun at Fort McKeen. Fort McKeen was an infantry post. With the establishment of Fort Abraham Lincoln, it was brought under that command. Courtesy of the SHSND

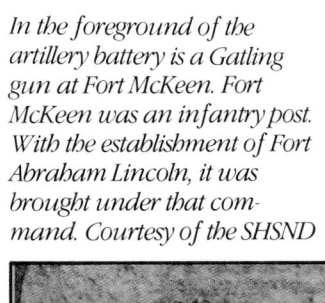

67

This was the brewery at Fort Abercrombie. Courtesy of the SHSND

Fort Abraham Lincoln had its own post trader. Alcoholism was recognized as a serious problem among both officers and enlisted men on frontier posts. Courtesy of the SHSND

A farewell "hop" was given in 1886 for retiring Col. Joseph N. G. Whister. The regimental flag is very similar to the North Dakota state flag. Such social events were a welcome relief for the officers and ladies of the fort. Courtesy of the SHSND

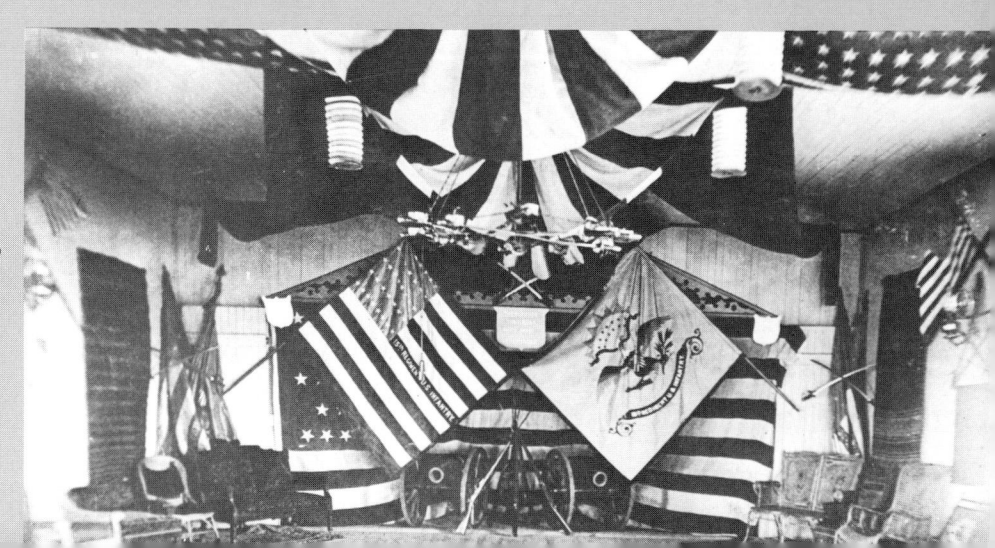

Soldiers were photographed while on a field exercise at Fort Pembina. Courtesy of the SHSND

The band of the Seventeenth Infantry posed at Fort Yates in 1883. Bands were important to frontier military life, and bandsmen were sometimes favored in duty assignments. Courtesy of the SHSND

Soldiers drilled at Fort Yates. Barracks are in the background. Courtesy of the SHSND

On July 19, 1881, Sitting Bull and 186 of his followers surrendered at Fort Buford. Refusing to agree to the terms offered following the military campaign against the Sioux in 1876, Sitting Bull and about four hundred followers retreated to Canada. Unable to eke out a living, the Sioux finally chose surrender over starvation. Courtesy of the SHSND

As with civilians, baseball was a favorite pastime for soldiers. The Fort Yates baseball team posed for this picture in 1890. Courtesy of the SHSND

...ing Bull's celebrity status to show business offers. In 85 he was persuaded to vel with the Buffalo Bill 'ld West show. Sitting Bull ly) posed together for this licity photo. Courtesy of SHSND

Although more than 100 Indian groups over a twenty-five-year period had accepted the Ghost Dance with little attendant violence, its practice at Standing Rock caused sufficient concern to order the arrest of Sitting Bull on December 15, 1890, by a detail of forty-three regular and special Indian Police led by Lt. Henry Bullhead. Courtesy of the SHSND

Graveside ceremonies were held on December 17, 1890, for the Indian police killed in the attempted arrest of Sitting Bull. Six Indian police died as did Sitting Bull and seven of his followers. Courtesy of the SHSND

RY IRVIN WRIGHT

Some of Sitting Bull's followers fled from Standing Rock and joined Big Foot and his band in South Dakota. On December 28, at Wounded Knee Creek, general fighting broke out following the discharge of a weapon during the process of disarming the Indians. Three hundred Sioux died. The period of conflict between the Sioux and the United States military ended on this tragic note. Courtesy of the SHSND

Fort Yates was the last of the frontier military posts to be abandoned (1903). In most cases the buildings were sold, moved away, or demolished. Only one post escaped destruction. Abandoned as a military post in 1890, Fort Totten operated as an Indian school until 1959. Courtesy of the SHSND

4

A United States land office opened in 1870 and the first entry made on public lands in North Dakota was by Charles Cavileer of Pembina. Joseph Rolette made a homestead entry at the same time and received the first patent for land. Cavileer's home, built in 1863 (shown here in a circa 1870 photo), also served as the first post office in the state. Courtesy of the SHSND

SETTLING NORTH DAKOTA 1870-1915

The television image of wagon trains carrying settlers to their new homes applies very little to North Dakota. The wagon trains of the 1860s carried gold-seekers through northern Dakota rather than to it. Steamboats were significant for carrying freight and passengers on the Missouri and Red rivers and across Devils Lake. But the transportation system which had the greatest effect on North Dakota—which settled North Dakota—was the railroad.

Dakota Territory was created in 1861, at that time comprising all of present-day North Dakota and South Dakota and most of Wyoming and Montana. These boundaries were modified until, in 1868, Dakota Territory came to include only the current states of North and South Dakota. Beginning in 1857 and 1858, townsite "boomers" had entered the territory in the extreme southeast corner, around Yankton. For the next twenty years most of the Dakota Territory's population would be within 100 miles of Yankton. By 1870, northern Dakota's non-Indian population was only 2,405, most of whom lived in the Saint Joseph-Pembina settlement in the northeast.

This changed rapidly, however. In 1869 the Hudson's Bay Company reached an agreement with the government in Ottawa whereby the Northwest would be united with the Dominion of Canada. The following year the province of Manitoba was created and a considerable immigration to that province from Ontario began. Because of the obstacles to travel between Manitoba and eastern Canada, that immigration took place through Minnesota and the Red River. From a population of twelve thousand in 1870, Manitoba grew to sixty-six thousand in 1881. This commerce on the Red River, including the addition of several steamboats during the 1870s, also promoted the settlement of the Red River Valley in Minnesota and northern Dakota. Moorhead became the head of navigation on the Red—until 1872 when a branch of the Saint Paul and Pacific Railroad reached Crookston, which in turn was replaced three years later by Fisher's Landing.

The railroad was not only moving up the Red River, it was also crossing it. In 1871 the Northern Pacific Railroad reached Moorhead, and squatters began to occupy land on the Dakota side of the Red River. By 1872, the year the Northern Pacific crossed into northern Dakota, claim shacks stretched from south of Fort Abercrombie to Grand Forks. A stage line ran from Fort Abercrombie to Pembina beginning in 1871, running on the east side of the river to Georgetown and then continuing up the west side of the river.

Each stage station spawned a small settlement. By June 1873 the Northern Pacific reached Bismarck leaving in its path settlements at Valley City (then called Worthington) and Jamestown. Construction stopped at Bismarck. Reckless spending and poor management sent the Northern Pacific into bankruptcy in September 1873. Jay Cooke, the famous financier who was selling the company's bonds, also lost his personal fortune and, in turn, his failure helped set off a national financial panic in 1873.

The Northern Pacific land grant was forty sections per mile, and the railroad was determined to attract settlers and sell this land. Although the efforts of the railroad (and to some extent of the territorial government) to encourage settlement did not produce great results during the early 1870s, during the period 1878 to 1890, growth was spectacular. In those twelve years the Euro-American population in northern Dakota grew from about 16,000 to 191,000 and North Dakota became a state. Euro-American civilization, with its towns, schools, and churches had been imposed on virgin plains. This growth reflected the growth of the United States as a whole, at that point experiencing rapid industrialization and immigration.

The railroads led the way for the boom. In 1878 James J. Hill and a group of partners took control of the Saint Paul and Pacific Railroad, and completed its lines in Minnesota from Crook-

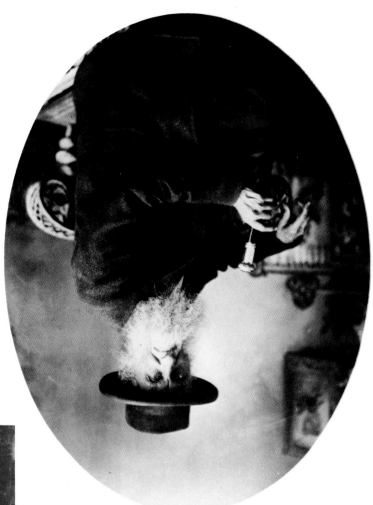

Charles Cavileer settled at Pembina, the area of the oldest Euro-American settlement in North Dakota, in 1851 as the first customs officer. He also served as postmaster for twenty-one years beginning in 1863. Courtesy of the SHSND

Most settlers and their possessions came to North Dakota by train, unloading at the depot nearest their destination. During the decade 1900 to 1910, when these unidentified settlers arrived, more than a quarter of a million people moved to North Dakota. As of 1910, approximately 45 percent of the state's population had lived here less than ten years. Courtesy of the SHSND

"Fargo on the Prairie," was the home of Gen. Thomas L. Rosser's Northern Pacific engineering crew and their families from 1871 to 1872. Meanwhile, a group of about six hundred squatters occupied "Fargo in the Timber," tents and cabins by the river to the east. A source of irritation to Rosser, the squatters were driven out by the military and the spring floods. Many subsequently moved to Valley City, Jamestown, and Bismarck as the railroad progressed. Courtesy of the SHSND

on to Saint Vincent and from Melrose to Alexandria, thereby linking up with the Canadian Pacific and completing the route from Minneapolis to Manitoba. This effort also saved the railroad's land grant. The following year the Saint Paul, Minneapolis, and Manitoba superseded the Saint Paul and Pacific and, under the management of Hill, began to expand significantly. The railroad expanded to Grand Forks in 1880, from there to Devils Lake in 1883. That same line was extended to Minot in 1886 and to Great Falls, Montana, in 1887. Other lines went north from Fargo through Grand Forks to Grafton, Saint Thomas, and Neche; west from Wahpeton; and north from Wahpeton through Casselton, Mayville, Larimore, Park River, and Langdon. The Northern Pacific, which had been stalled at Bismarck, crossed the Missouri in 1879 and the line to the Pacific was completed in 1883. Total railroad mileage in North Dakota increased from 900 miles in 1878 to 2,093 in 1890.

Settlers poured into North Dakota, lured by promise of cheap and free land in advertising put out by the Northern Pacific, by land dealers, and by the territorial government, the last having the smallest impact. The Northern Pacific had agents in the eastern United States and in northern Europe and the British Isles. Many settlers arrived in colonies. Most of the settlers in this period arrived from other states, with Minnesota, Wisconsin, and New York providing the largest

numbers. Of the more than 81,000 foreign-born in North Dakota in 1890, the largest numbers were from Norway (25,773) and Canada (23,045). Other significant numbers of immigrants had arrived from Germany, England, Ireland, Sweden, and Russia. Towns sprang up rapidly—virtually overnight—usually with the expectation that each would grow into a metropolis. Speculators platted other townsites with great hope, envisioning great profits from selling lots, but the towns existed in name only without a lot being sold or a building constructed.

The increasing population of the northern part of Dakota Territory brought about political changes as well. Yankton's leaders feared the railroad's influence. The growth of the railroads also served to divide the Territory between north and south. Grain millers and other Saint Paul and Minneapolis business interests had strong economic ties to the Red River Valley and the rest of northern Dakota. In a move which outraged Yankton's citizens, the territorial legislature created a Capitol Commission in 1883 to choose a new site for the capitol of Dakota Territory. On June 2, 1883, the commission decided on Bismarck, and construction on the capitol began that year. Henry Villard, president of the Northern Pacific Railroad, laid the cornerstone for the new building during a brief stop on his "Gold Spike Excursion" to Gold Creek, Montana, marking the completion of the Northern Pacific's trans-

continental route.

Desire for statehood followed from the southern Dakota leaders, while the railroad interests in northern Dakota resisted, finding it easier to control territorial appointments from Washington. Finally, with both Republicans and Democrats voting in favor, Congress passed the Omnibus Bill of February 22, 1889, which authorized North Dakota, South Dakota, Montana, and Washington to frame constitutions and submit them for ratification. North Dakota's constitutional convention opened in Bismarck on July 4, 1889, with seventy-five members. In addition to providing the framework for state government, the constitution also established the locations of the state's institutions. The capitol and the penitentiary were already in place in Bismarck, although the capitol's location would be a source of contention for years to come. The university was at Grand Forks and the hospital for the insane was at Jamestown. Although no appropriations had ever been made, the territorial legislature had established an agricultural college at Fargo. To protect these and to satisfy the rest of the new state, normal schools were placed at Mayville and Valley City, a reform school at Mandan, a school of science at Wahpeton, a school for the deaf at Devils Lake, a school for the blind in Pembina County, an industrial school at Ellendale, a soldiers' home at Lisbon, and a school of forestry to be located in Rolette, Ward, McHenry, or Bottineau counties. Historian Elwyn B. Robinson characterized this large number of institutions (along with the large number of towns, high railroad mileage, and other items requiring support and consuming investment) as part of the "too much mistake" in North Dakota history. In effect, too many institutions to support by too few people. This was caused, according to Robinson, by immigrants from an environment which would support a larger population not understanding the need to adapt to this new, semiarid environment which would not adequately support these institutions.

The new constitution was ratified overwhelmingly. Approved by a much closer margin was a separate article prohibiting the sale and consumption of alcoholic beverages. On November 2, 1889, North Dakota became a state. John Miller became the first governor. The first legislature met beginning November 19, and over the next 120 days passed 201 laws, many of them routine in nature—defining the duties of state officials, establishing the structure of local government, and so forth. But 14 dealt with the grain trade and with railroads. No issue in North Dakota's history has been more significant than the power of the railroads and the elevator companies over the economic life of North Dakotans. As just one example, when the Interstate Commerce Commission was created in 1887, the first complaint received by the new federal agency was from farmers in Pembina County complaining about railroad rates. And in fact the power of the railroads and the elevator companies was enormous. Directly, they controlled prices and freight rates. Although seemingly in competition, the Northern Pacific and the Great Northern railroads had come to agreement on branch line and rates in 1882. Less directly, they wielded gre[at] political power, most notably through the political machine of Alexander McKenzie, agent for the Northern Pacific Railroad.

As North Dakota began its existence as a state, however, the glorious economic expansion of the previous decade had stopped. Hard times se[t] in. The boom had actually ended a few years before statehood, largely because it had been fueled by speculation which could not be sustained. In 1890 many of the recent settlers were frightened by rumors of imminent Indian attack. The governor was bombarded with requests for weapons, and local militia prepared for an imagined massacre.

The tragedy which did occur largely befell the Indians with such events as the death of Sitting Bull in December 1890, and the infamous battle at Wounded Knee in South Dakota. The state

Although the Northern Pacific crossed the Missouri River in 1879, a bridge across the river was not completed until 1883. In the meantime, the train had to be ferried across. In winter, tracks were laid on the ice and the train crossed on a bridge of ice. On at least one occasion, the ice did not hold. Courtesy of the SHSND

The bridge over the Red River is shown here as it appeared in 1872, shortly after the Northern Pacific crossed into northern Dakota. Moorhead and Fargo also served as the departure point for river traffic going north. Courtesy of the SHSND

Great Northern construction taking place in 1887. Courtesy of the SHSND

The discovery of gold in the Black Hills and its confirmation by a military expedition under the command of Gen. George Custer in 1874 created new customers for the Northern Pacific's line to Bismarck. Passengers could then take a stage coach from Bismarck to Deadwood. The railroad also connected with steamboats moving both up and down the Missouri River. Courtesy of the SHSND

Upon completion of the railroad bridge across the Missouri River at Bismarck in September 1883, the Northern Pacific tested its strength with eight Mogul engines. Below, steamboats continued to ply the river (boat landing in lower portion of picture), maintaining active commerce on the Missouri until well into the twentieth century. Courtesy of the SHSND

As the railroad moved west, the little town of Medora became a favorite jumping off point for the Black Hills. Courtesy of the SHSND

ered through drought in 1891. In 1893 the ion as a whole suffered through economic iculties. In 1892 North Dakota elected a oulist governor, Eli C. D. Shortridge, in an ort to force the railroads and the elevator npanies to reform. These efforts met with ited success, and in 1895 a conservative oublican, Roger Allin, again was in the gover-'s office.

Although the state continued to face financial iculties as the decade progressed, by the end he 1890s a new boom was underway, again ecting the growth of the United States as a ole. Between 1898 and 1915, 367,000 more ople settled in the state and railroad mileage arly doubled to 5,226 miles. The population of rth Dakota reached 637,000 in 1915, but only reased by 10,000 in the next five years, to ,000. Between 1900 and 1910 the number of ns grew from 45,000 to 74,000. The number of es planted into wheat doubled between 1898 1915. Prices for farm products rose during s period and rainfall was adequate. As a result, ny new farmers settled on the Missouri teau, farming it as intensively as they would Red River Valley. Wheat was king.

In 1910, as immigration to North Dakota was at its peak, seven out of every ten North Dakotans were either foreign-born or had parents who were foreign-born. The largest number of foreign immigrants in the decade 1900 to 1910 had come from Russia, largely Germans from Russia, followed closely by a continuing influx of immigrants from Norway. More than one in five North Dakotans had been born in Norway or had parents who had been born in Norway. More than one in ten were born or had parents who were born in Russia, and about the same number made the same claim in respect to Germany. As of 1910 the countries which had provided the greatest numbers of settlers to the state (foreign-born or foreign-born parents) were, in order: Norway, Russia, Germany, Canada, Sweden, Denmark, Ireland, Austria, England, Hungary, Scotland, Finland, Holland, Switzerland, Romania, Italy, Greece, France, Turkey, Belgium, and Bulgaria. Although 70 percent had foreign parentage, only a little more than one in four had themselves been born in another country. More than a third of the state's people had been born in North Dakota by 1910.

In their modest beginnings, Grand Forks in 1876 did not look appreciably different from Bismarck in that same year. Both were rough frontier towns. Courtesy of the SHSND

Bismarck, (as it appeared in 1873, the year the Northern Pacific Railroad arrived), contained establishments offering "wine, women, cards, anything that corrupt men or bad women would be apt to seek." In the fall of 1873, after a soldier was killed by a regular patron of Mullen and O'Neill's Dance Hall, soldiers raided the town, killing Mullen and wounding a bartender. Courtesy of the SHSND

Unlike Fargo, Bismarck, and other cities which sprang up as the railroads came through (or in anticipation of their coming), Grand Forks was founded as a result of traffic on the Red River. Established in 1870 by Capt. Alexander Griggs, Grand Forks boasted a population of 1,705 when the Saint Paul, Minneapolis, and Manitoba Railroad (Great Northern) reached it in 1880. The steamer Selkirk is shown docked at Third Street in 1882, a feat made possible by extensive flooding of the Red River. James J. Hill placed the Selkirk in service in 1871. Courtesy of the SHSND

The J. L. Grandin, *the first Dakota built and owned steamboat, was placed in service on April 27, 1878. One of three steamboats owned by the Grandin brothers, owners of the Grandin bonanza farm, the* J. L. Grandin *was the largest tonnage displacement vessel used on the Red River. The Grandins owned four miles of frontage on the river and were able to move their wheat by river to Fargo, where it could be shipped by rail. The Grandins owned over one hundred sections of land. Courtesy of the SHSND*

The steamboat Washburn *unloaded a Case steam tractor at an unknown landing on the Missouri River. Hauling freight on the Missouri continued well into the twentieth century. Courtesy of the SHSND*

This is an interior view of the freight house at the Missouri River landing in Bismarck, shown here in about 1900. Originally, the freight house was seven hundred feet long, with the river on one side and the Northern Pacific tracks on the other. Tracks (removed before this picture was taken) for freight transfer trams ran through the building. Courtesy of the SHSND

85

Winter storms occasionally delayed railroad traffic—sometimes with drifts higher than the train. This light-hearted group of passengers stuck near Mohall in January 1907 decided to have some fun with their predicament. January 1907 was an extremely cold, stormy month. The snowfall averaged 14.5 inches across the state and Kulm received 34.5 inches. Heavy snow and winds caused numerous delays. Another group, stuck at Sheyenne during a storm that month, were immortalized in a newspaper published while the group was snowbound. The one and only edition of the Sheyenne Blizzard, *"Skiddo Edition," appeared on January 23, 1907. Courtesy of the SHSND*

With the completion of the Northern Pacific line, the railroad organized a "Gold Spike" excursion across the route carrying dignitaries which included Northern Pacific President Henry Villard and former President Ulysses S. Grant. As Henry Villard and his party passed through Bismarck, they participated in laying the cornerstone of the new capitol of Dakota Territory on September 5, 1883. The capitol had been removed from Yankton based on the decision of a commission which toured several towns in the territory. It had to convene on a moving train to avoid hostile crowds in Yankton. Courtesy of the SHSND

The Legislative Assembly was in session in the first North Dakota Capitol. Courtesy of the SHSND

Alexander McKenzie, agent for the Northern Pacific Railroad, was a member of the Capitol Commission. Although the only elective office McKenzie ever held was sheriff of Burleigh County, he headed a powerful political machine which dominated North Dakota politics for many years. Courtesy of the SHSND

The North Dakota Constitutional Convention opened with a parade in Bismarck on July 4, 1889. Courtesy of the SHSND

Most farmers began farming with horses or oxen and, although North Dakota farms tended to be larger than in the eastern United States, most were not bonanzas. The average farm in 1920 was 466 acres. Courtesy of the SHSND

North Dakota agriculture did tend to be more mechanized, a trend that has continued throughout the state's history. In 1909 more than three-fifths of the state's land area was in farms, and three-fifths of the value of all crops was represented by wheat. Courtesy of the SHSND

The bankruptcy of the Northern Pacific Railroad made large amounts of land available to holders of the company's securities at a very low price. The Cass-Cheney farm, later the Dalrymple farm, was the first bonanza farm. Purchased in 1874, the farm is estimated to have had up to sixty-five thousand acres under cultivation at one time. Taking advantage of cheap land, the bonanzas used mechanization and professional management to produce vast amounts of wheat. Courtesy of the SHSND

Gov. John Burke posed with William Jennings Bryan in Fargo, September 1, 1908. Burke, the state's first Democratic governor, was elected with the support of progressive Republicans, representing the end of the McKenzie machine. Burke served from 1907 to 1912. Courtesy of the SHSND

This 1880 photo depicts workers threshing in the Red River Valley. Courtesy of the SHSND

Bucking and stacking hay on the Johnson Land and Cattle Company farm, Oakes, was photographed in the early 1900s. Courtesy of the SHSND

Cutting and shocking grain on the David C. Herndon farm in Nelson County was captured in this photo. Field work often involved the whole family, and threshing usually involved the combined efforts of several farmers. Courtesy of the SHSND

This farmer is shown hauling one thousand bushels of flax to the elevator in Beach, about 1903. Flax was another major crop used to promote the state. Farmers were advised that they could pay for their land in one year by raising flax. Courtesy of the SHSND

Farmers were long encouraged to diversify and move away from a dependence on raising wheat. One of the "new" crops was potatoes, here promoted with a special train of fifty cars loading at Berthold and destined for eastern states. Courtesy of the SHSND

Farmers lined up at the elevator to sell their harvest. The control of railroads and line elevators over the grading and pricing of crops was a major cause for both political and economic organizing in the state, leading to the formation of cooperatives and to such political movements as the Populists and the Nonpartisan League. Courtesy of the SHSND

Although the buffalo were almost extinct, the residue from their slaughter littered the prairie. Settlers found a ready cash crop harvesting bones which were used to make fertilizer. Courtesy of the SHSND

Wagonloads of bones lined up on Main Street in Minot in 1888 to be shipped east on the Saint Paul, Minneapolis and Manitoba Railroad (the next year the line would become the Great Northern). Through 1889, 6,730 tons of buffalo bones were shipped from Minot alone, probably representing the remains of more than a quarter of a million animals. The bones brought about nine dollars a ton. Courtesy of the SHSND

Percheron mares were a common sight on the Usher Burdick farm near Munich. Burdick also rounded up and tamed wild horses for sale. The number of horses on farms grew throughout this period, climbing from 359,948 in 1900 to 855,682 in 1920. Courtesy of the SHSND

Survey parties went in advance of the settlers, marking the lands which settlers would claim. Upon finding land which he or she wanted to claim, the would-be homesteader registered at the Government Land Office. An individual could claim 160 acres for the cost of a filing fee of eighteen dollars to twenty-two dollars. Settlement had to start within six months and had to continue for five years, at which time the claim was proved up. The homesteader could also secure title after fourteen months by paying cash and making proof of settlement. Courtesy of the SHSND

The settler's first home was often a tarpaper shack, built of sawed lumber and covered with tarpaper to keep out the wind and the accompanying dirt or snow. Regulations for homesteading required a dwelling to be at least twelve by fourteen feet. Courtesy of the SHSND

The scarcity of trees, the cost of lumber, and the abundance of sod made the latter an attractive building material for homes on the prairie. Some sod houses were much more elaborate than others. Courtesy of the SHSND

Sod was a building material which produced a structure much warmer in winter and cooler in summer than the typical wooden claim shack. The structure was sometimes built in two parts, housing the family in one part and live-stock in the other. The Christ Geier home was near Linton. Courtesy of the SHSND

Shown here is a sod home near Jamestown. Courtesy of the SHSND

Much of the land which enticed settlers to North Dakota was not free homestead land, but land for sale through land companies. Much of this land had been purchased from the Northern Pacific Railroad. This group of landseekers in 1903 is departing from Medina for a tour of the Hackney-Boyton Land Company properties. Photo from The Record

The railroads often organized groups of colonies of individuals to settle in the state. This photo was taken by the Great Northern Railway of a group of 350 Church of the Brethren members as they passed through Saint Paul on their way from Indiana to Ramsey County in 1894. Two years later a similar train brought 1,036 more colonists from Indiana. That train was comprised of nineteen coaches and over one hundred freight cars. Courtesy of the SHSND

Land companies used every imaginable pitch to sell their lands. The William H. Brown Company, with extensive holdings in Morton County, implied that there was an overabundance of women in the state by circulating this photo of a class at Flasher Public School with the caption, "Nine of these girls will have no husbands." In fact, there were about 120 men for every one hundred women in the state. Courtesy of the SHSND

Building materials varied from logs, where available, to sod, cut lumber, stones and brick. Courtesy of the SHSND

Two unidentified women posed with their pets for this charming photograph. Courtesy of the SHSND

Although often rough-looking on the outside, sod house interiors could present a warm and inviting atmosphere as in this 1907 photograph. Courtesy of the SHSND

These women were photographed at the Robert Bailey home, Sutton, in 1904 while tearing up rags in order to make rugs. Courtesy of the SHSND

The Frank D. Hughes home at Arvilla provided a luxurious contrast to many early homes in North Dakota. Mr. Hughes is shown standing on the steps, Mrs. Hughes is sitting on the chair, and their daughter is seated on the railing. Courtesy of the SHSND

A Saint Paul, Minneapolis, and Manitoba Railway (Great Northern) train at Arvilla station was photographed about 1882 or 1883. Arvilla was founded by Frank D. Hughes and Dudley H. Hersey. The Hughes and Hersey lumberyard is in the background in the far left of the photograph. Courtesy of the SHSND

Young photographer Frank Fiske of Fort Yates shows off a number of his prints in his studio on "finishing day." Photo studios relied on natural light and usually had large skylight windows. The huge camera to the right of the window took pictures on eight inch by ten inch glass plates. Courtesy of the SHSND

Towns sprung up quickly during the boom periods. Bathgate, incorporated in 1882 and shown here between 1886 and 1889, boasted a number of businesses, including a photographer. James F. Derby, who undoubtedly took this photograph which included his place of business, was already the second photographer to have set up business here. He and druggist Samuel T. Witmer shared this location and advertised together. The Bathgate Dakota Bank is in the far left of the photo, and Joseph J. Auger's general store is barely visible at the right. Courtesy of the SHSND

The sale of town lots, as pictured here at Bowman on November 21, 1907, usually drew a crowd and good prices as speculators pictured the next metropolis on the prairie. Courtesy of the SHSND

"Mott's the Spot!" became a well-recognized promotional phrase. Mott is pictured here between 1905 and 1910. Courtesy of the SHSND

In April 1897, rapid melting of the winter's heavy snowfall caused extensive flooding with the greatest damage taking place along the Red River. In Grand Forks about twenty-five blocks of paving were under water, with the water three feet higher than in 1882, when a steamboat landed on Third Street. Settlers had to adjust to the whims of nature, which often included flooding in the vicinity of rivers and in the flat land of the Red River Valley. This photo was taken in the streets of Hillsboro. Courtesy of the SHSND

B. H. Smith Wagon Shop and
Blacksmithing was located in
Steele. Many such shops
adapted to the times, repairing
early automobiles and mechanized farm equipment.
Courtesy of the SHSND

Shown here is the interior of
the Rock Lake General Store.
Courtesy of the SHSND

The Krem Roller Mill was photographed about 1904. As elsewhere, manufacturing moved in the direction of fewer and larger units. Between 1909 and 1914, the number of flour mills and gristmills dropped from eighty-four to fifty-nine and the number of people employed went from 435 to 424. However, the value of products produced increased. In 1914 North Dakota ranked thirty-seventh among the states in population, but forty-sixth in value of manufactured products and forty-eighth in average number of wage earners. Courtesy of the SHSND

This slaughterhouse was located in Jamestown. Courtesy of the SHSND

Farmers lined up at the Krem Creamery about 1906. Sales of cream and eggs by smaller diversified farms provided regular cash income between harvests until recent times. Receipts from the sale of cream, butter, and butter fat each far exceeded the value of milk sold in North Dakota. In 1909, the value of cream sold in the state was $528,977, while receipts from milk were only $293,956. Courtesy of the SHSND

When the Northern Pacific Railroad opened the Missouri Slope, the earliest visitors to that country saw its great potential for raising cattle. Some of the early cattlemen had come to the region to hunt, but had become enthusiastic at the thought of becoming cattle barons. Streams, plentiful grasses, and coulees and ravines which provided protection for the animals brought the ranching frontier to North Dakota. Courtesy of the SHSND

This winter street scene was taken in Granville, McHenry County. Courtesy of the SHSND

This is how the offices of the weekly Williston Graphic appeared in 1903, one of 228 newspapers then publishing in the state. Over the course of the state's history, more than thirteen hundred titles of newspapers have been published in North Dakota. The repository of news, opinions, and dreams, local newspapers often boosted the town, sometimes tried to reform it, and occasionally engaged in journalistic wars with rival towns or with rival papers across the street. Today fewer than one hundred newspapers continue to publish.

In 1909 the census reported 330 printing and publishing establishments in the state, employing 788 individuals. Nearly one-third of all printing and publishing establishments were located in Fargo and Grand Forks at that time. In fact, Fargo and Grand Forks in 1914, with only 4.5 percent of the state's population, accounted for 22.8 percent of the state's manufactured goods. Courtesy of the SHSND

Initially drawn to the Little Missouri area to hunt, twenty-five-year-old Theodore Roosevelt decided to go into ranching in the fall of 1883. Although he invested a considerable sum of money, $82,500, Roosevelt, like many of the other ranchers, was a squatter, not holding title to land at either the Maltese Cross Ranch or the Elkhorn Ranch. Courtesy of the SHSND

Herds foraged for themselves, roaming the grasslands. The annual roundup brought long hours in the saddle and often, bad weather, damp beds, and wet clothes. The first roundup on the Little Missouri was held in 1884. Courtesy of the SHSND

A. C. Huidekoper, who had come out from Pennsylvania on a hunting trip in 1881, set up the Little Missouri Horse Company (the Headquarters Ranch is shown here in the late summer of 1892) and the HT Ranch in 1884. Huidekoper ranched until, bitter over the homesteading of the rangeland, he sold his herd of four thousand horses in 1905. Courtesy of the SHSND

Cowboys lined up for breakfast from the Marquis de Mores chuckwagon during roundup in 1885. Courtesy of the SHSND

About to start on a hunting trip, the Marquis de Mores (standing in foreground) and Medora (seated sidesaddle) posed by the chateau. Antoine Amedee Marie Vincent Manca de Vallombrosa, the Marquis de Mores, continues to be, along with Theodore Roosevelt, the most celebrated resident of the Missouri Slope in this era. Married to the wealthy Medora Von Hoffman, the young French aristocrat founded the town of Medora in April 1883. By the following January, the little boom town had eighty-four buildings, including three hotels. Courtesy of the SHSND

The Marquis built a meat-packing plant at Medora with the plan to ship refrigerated beef east. (Shown here are the cooling house and loading platform.) He also built a twenty-eight-room chateau (now a state historic site), a church and a school, and backed other businesses. His businesses failed; the packing plant closed in November 1886, and by 1889 the town of Medora was largely deserted. Courtesy of the SHSND

This photo was taken of Medora in 1885. The packing plant with its chimney is in the right-hand portion of the picture. Courtesy of the SHSND

In 1898, the Berry-Boise Cattle Company closed out, shipping about 7,500 head of cattle from yards four miles west of Dickinson. Although many of the large cattle outfits left as the range was homesteaded, cattle numbers continued to increase in the state. The census reported over 281,000 head in 1890, 657,000 head in 1900, 743,000 in 1910, and 1.3 million in 1920. Courtesy of the SHSND

A. C. Huidekoper, seated center, posed for this photo at HT Ranch logging camp. Courtesy of the SHSND

113

About twenty-two head went into each car and each train pulled about twenty-five cars. Courtesy of the SHSND

Sheep numbers dropped significantly after 1900, as the Slope region filled with homesteaders. The state had 681,952 sheep on its farms in 1900, but only 293,371 in 1910 and 298,912 in 1920. Courtesy of the SHSND

Wool production was reported at over three million pounds in 1899 and just under 1.7 million pounds in 1909. Wool is being hauled into Dickinson in this photo. Courtesy of the SHSND

North Dakota's cities expanded and contracted with the state's economy. Fargo, the largest city in the state, fell in population from 7,394 in 1885 to 5,664 in 1890 after the first Dakota boom fizzled. By 1900, the population had climbed to 9,589. Although still a town of largely wooden buildings, this view of Broadway before the Great Fire of 1893 shows several brick structures. Courtesy of the SHSND

On a hot June 3, 1893, a fire, supposedly originating from a pan of hot ashes discarded from a restaurant, spread east and north from Front Street in Fargo. Before it ended, it burned over 160 acres of the city, destroyed more than one hundred businesses and caused an estimated three million dollars in losses. Fargo rebuilt and within two years was celebrating an annual Fire Festival. Similar fires devastated other North Dakota towns as well. Courtesy of the SHSND

Two unidentified men posed with the Scranton Fire Department pumper. Courtesy of the SHSND

The Hillsboro Fire Department Running Team of 1894 participated in a hose race at an association meeting. Courtesy of the SHSND

With the invention of the "safety" bicycle, a bicycle craze seized the country in the 1890s. Fargo claimed the largest bicycle dealer in the Northwest in the George D. Brown dealership, distributing the "Syracuse Crimson Rim" brand, the choice of the Fargo and Moorhead police departments according to Brown's advertising. Courtesy of the SHSND

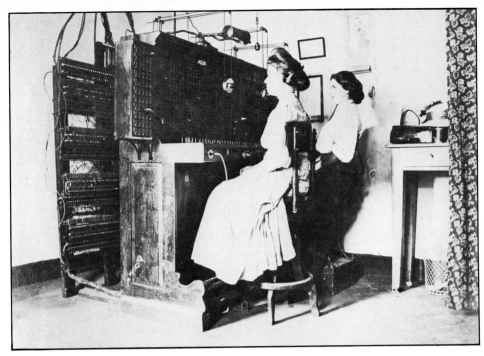

Unidentified telephone operators staffed this switchboard. The settlement period saw considerable modernization. Telephone cooperatives were started in many rural areas. Courtesy of the SHSND

The United States declared war on Spain on April 25, 1898. Within three days, Gov. Frank Briggs was notified that the quota for the state was eight companies of infantry. Within a month the First North Dakota was bound for San Francisco and ultimately, the Philippines. Company I, from Wahpeton, and Company K, from Dickinson, are pictured. United States Secretary of State John Hay referred to it as a "splendid little war." The United States armed forces were successful and although the military leadership proved to be scandalously inept, the soldiers performed well. One of the worst scandals of the war was the high number of soldiers who lost their lives to disease—more than ten times as many as died from bullets. Fifteen North Dakotans were killed. Courtesy of the SHSND

North Dakota's soldiers distinguished themselves in the Spanish-American War. Especially notable were the actions of Company G, Valley City, shown here in front of their quarters at Malate, Philippines. Their daring in crossing a burning bridge at San Isidro while under enemy fire is recognized to this day by the National Guard. Two members of this company, Sterling Galt and Charles P. Davis, received medals of honor. Courtesy of the SHSND

117

*Rodeos have provided enter-
taiment throughout the state's
history. This scene from the
State Fair at Mandan in 1897
was used to advertise the 1898
event. Among the attractions
was the Marquis De Mores's
statecoach, which "will be held
up by genuine Indians and
cowboys. The stagecoach will
be burned by the Indians. . . . "
Courtesy of the SHSND*

STATE FAIR MANDAN, N. D.

September 27-28-29-30, 1898.

*Baseball has always been a
favorite pastime. Most small
towns fielded a team, and
games drew enthusiastic
crowds as did this game at
New England early in the
century. Courtesy of the
SHSND*

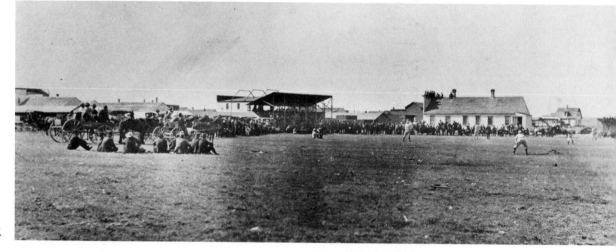

*This picnic at Bowman was
photographed on July 4, 1908.
Courtesy of the SHSND*

Opera houses, actually auditoriums, were more likely to have a minstrel show or other popular entertainment of the day rather than an opera. This photo was taken at the Williston Opera House. Courtesy of the SHSND

The Forman Gunclub was photographed September 2, 1908. Successful hunts offered numerous opportunities to have photographs taken to commemorate the event, including studio shots. Courtesy of the SHSND

This group from McLean County hunted in the Badlands for two weeks when this picture was taken in 1904. Courtesy of the SHSND

Speakers at Chautauqua assemblies disseminated ideas in an informal, relaxing setting. The state's premier Chautauqua grounds were on Devils Lake, opening in July 1893. With a half mile of lake frontage, more than one hundred acres of land, a three-story hotel, camp grounds, one-thousand-seat auditorium, and other amenities, the grounds was a major vacation and recreation area. The Minnie H., piloted by Captain Heerman, here landing at the Chautauqua grounds, provided trips on the lake. A railroad also ran between the grounds and the city. Courtesy of the SHSND

A railroad ran between the Chautaqua grounds and the city of Devils Lake. Courtesy of the SHSND

Rowboats were available for rental at the Chautauqua, and the grounds included a bicycle track, lawn tennis court, croquet ground, and baseball diamond. As the twentieth century progressed, the automobile doomed the small Chautaqua railroad and low water ruined the recreational appeal of Devils Lake. Courtesy of the SHSND

A quilting party took place at the Pendroy family home in McHenry County in 1888. The quilt pattern is a double Irish chain. Courtesy of the SHSND

Many northern Dakota towns had an early "wide-open" reputation. One particular concern of the reformers was liquor traffic. Temperence advocates march down a Devils Lake street in the late 1880s. Prohibition was approved by the voters of North Dakota in 1889 and added to the state's constitution. Courtesy of the SHSND

Illegal liquor establishments or "blind pigs" operated in spite of the ban. This establishment was located at White Earth about 1902. Courtesy of the SHSND

The Keeley Institute of Fargo, founded in 1894, was one of several centers established by Dr. Keeley for the treatment of alcohol and drug addiction. Alcohol and drug abuse were recognized as serious problems at the time. In its first five years of operation the Fargo facility claimed six hundred cures, and the organization's operations nationally claimed "over three hundred thousand men and women cured of the whiskey, morphine and tobacco addictions" since 1880. Courtesy of the SHSND

This 1913 photo shows Brooklyn School, located in Williams County. The school buses were placed on sleigh runners in the winter. Some were closed and even carried a small stove, but all were cold in winter. Courtesy of the SHSND

Students face the camera in Michigan, Nelson County. In 1910, 80.7 percent of children in the state, ages six to fourteen attended school. By counties, the percentage ranged from a high of 88.9 percent in Traill County to 54.9 percent in McIntosh County. The percentage of children in school dropped off sharply after age fourteen. Whereas 90 percent of all ten to fourteen year olds were in school, only 57 percent of those age fifteen to seventeen were in school in 1910. Courtesy of the SHSND

The old president's house at the University of North Dakota, Grand Forks, is shown with the trolley running in front. The University of North Dakota predates the state, being established as part of the bargain which sent the Dakota Territory Capitol to Bismarck. The University held its first classes in 1884-1885, with a total of 79 students enrolled. Since there were few high schools in the state, most of the early students were enrolled in the preparatory department. In 1888-89, 179 students were enrolled in the preparatory department; only 20 were enrolled as college students.

With statehood, additional institutions were added. The Agricultural College at Fargo and the normal schools at Valley City and Mayville started in 1890. Ellendale Normal School opened in 1899, the School of Science at Wahpeton in 1904, the School of Forestry at Bottineau in 1907, the normal school at Minot in 1913, and the normal school at Dickinson in 1918. The last two schools were authorized by constitutional amendments while the remainder were in the original 1889 Constitution. Courtesy SHSND

School was held in a variety of structures. The student body of Gamache School is ready for a baseball game. Courtesy of the SHSND

The availability of lignite coal for fuel was used as a selling point by land companies luring settlers to western North Dakota. The use of lignite to fuel a blacksmith forge was reported to have occurred with the Lewis and Clark expedition, and commercial mining began early in the 1880s in Ward County, along the Mouse River. Shown here is the Bob Miller coal mine near Williston about 1902. Courtesy of the SHSND

The Washburn Lignite Coal Company, started in 1900, operated one of the largest underground mines in North Dakota near Wilton. Shown here about 1901, the mine employed four hundred men in 1915. However, most mining operations were small. Two of the more than one hundred mines operating in 1919 employed 46 percent of the wage-earning miners. Courtesy of the SHSND

The Washburn Lignite Coal Company used advertising to promote its coal. Courtesy of the SHSND

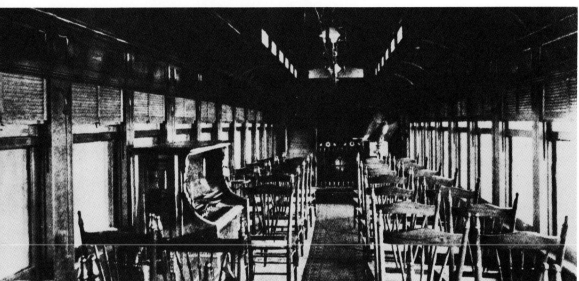

The Cathedral Car of North Dakota, the brainchild of Episcopal Bishop W. D. Walker, testified to the vast spaces of the state as well as to its extensive railroad network. Religious services were held on sidings at towns across the state, with railway workers reportedly taking special care to park the car at a relatively quiet spot. The idea was copied not only by other religious denominations in this country, but also in other countries around the world. Courtesy of the SHSND

Frikirke Bygget (Free Church Building) was located in Sheyenne township, (Richland County, 1912). Settlers in North Dakota brought their institutions with them; churches with immigrant members often conducted services in foreign languages. Each denomination attempted to serve its members throughout the state and many small churches were formed. As of 1916, the Methodist, Presbyterian, Baptist, Congregational, and Episcopal churches averaged only forty-eight members per congregation, while the Lutherans averaged seventy-two members and the Roman Catholics averaged 252. Everyone expected the great growth of the settlement period to continue and built accordingly, anticipating a future in which, as the first Catholic bishop of North Dakota, John Shanley, wrote, "We can expect to see North Dakota as thickly settled as Pennsylvania." Courtesy of the SHSND

This photo was taken of Burleigh County draftees in 1917. More than 160,000 men were registered for the draft in North Dakota during World War I, and 31,269 served in the armed forces. Of those that served, 19,772 volunteered and the remainder were drafted. The first to go overseas were the National Guard regiments numbering 4,195 officers and enlisted men.

Having survived his first battle in the trenches of France, Harry Rosten of the 137th Infantry, American Expeditionary Force, wrote home to a friend in Roseglen: "I pity the poor gophers you and I shot last summer, but then, they at least had a hole they could dodge into." Courtesy of the SHSND

5

WAR AND DEPRESSION 1915-1940

The decade and a half preceding World War I witnessed a progressive movement in the United States, which also had a profound effect on North Dakota. Reform was varied. Edwin Ladd, professor at the North Dakota Agricultural College and chemist at the experiment station, led the fight against adulterated food and other adulterated or contaminated consumer products. In 1906, progressive forces of Republicans and Democrats elected Democrat John Burke as governor, marking the beginning of the end for the McKenzie machine. North Dakota's most significant contribution to national politics, however, was the Nonpartisan League, which Arthur C. Townley organized in 1915. Using a genius for organizing and capitalizing on the farmer's feelings of exploitation, the League swept through the state like a prairie fire, capturing first the Republican party in the June 1916 primary election, and then going on to take virtually all state offices in the general election, as well as a majority in the state House of Representatives. The NPL gained control of both houses of the Legislative Assembly in 1919, and with Lynn J. Frazier as governor, the League began to enact a program of state industries. Opposition to the League, in the form of the Independent Voters Association or IVA, attacked the NPL leadership as being disloyal in the war and the League's program as socialistic and un-American. Frazier, Attorney General William Lemke, and commissioner of Agriculture and Labor John N. Hagen were removed from office through a recall election on October 28, 1921, but the League legacy lived on in such creations as the Bank of North Dakota and the State Mill and Elevator. For the next forty years as well, the key electoral contests in the state would be in the primary election within the Republican party.

The free land in the state was almost gone when war broke out in Europe in the summer of 1914. The state's population grew slowly for the remainder of the decade. North Dakotans generally opposed U.S. involvement in the war, and supported the reelection of President Woodrow Wilson in 1916 as he campaigned on the slogan, "He kept us out of war." In 1917 the United States did enter the war, however, and North Dakotans supported the war effort. More than thirty-one thousand people served in the military, and the state oversubscribed to each Liberty Loan drive. The hysteria and trampling of individual liberties that accompanied the war were not as pronounced in North Dakota, thanks in part to the courage of Judge Charles F. Amidon. Still, ugly

This was a World War I poster. Films, posters, and speakers were all used to inspire patriotic fervor. Courtesy of the SHSND

Returning soldiers were welcomed at Fort Yates in 1919. Of the more than thirty-five thousand claims for exemption or deferment the state draft board considered in 1918, none came from able-bodied Sioux from Standing Rock.

World War I claimed the lives of 1,176 soldiers from North Dakota, an extraordinarily high number when compared to other wars in this century. In fact, as many died from disease as from combat. Returning soldiers received a bonus from the state of twenty-five dollars a month for every month of service. Courtesy of the SHSND

One of the favorite diversions of soldiers in training (at least when cameras were present) was the blanket toss, here performed for visitors at Fort Lincoln, Bismarck, in 1917. Courtesy of the SHSND

Arthur Charles Townley spoke at Crosby in 1916. The thirty-five-year-old Townley led the Nonpartisan League to victory that year as the organization captured the state House of Representatives and most state offices. The League was Townley's most striking achievement in a life otherwise largely filled with failure. Still remembered by many North Dakotans, Townley, who died in 1959, remains a controversial figure. Courtesy of the SHSND

This NPL picnic was held in Ward County on July 4, 1916. The goat, "the animal that fights with its head," was the symbol of the Nonpartisan League. The League went on from its wins in 1916 to almost complete victory in 1918, capturing both houses of the Legislative Assembly and allowing the party to enact its program, "The New Day in North Dakota." Courtesy of the SHSND

SOME LEAKS IN THE PIPE LINE

FATHERS, MOTHERS, WHAT DO YOU THINK OF IT?

The "Direct Pipe Line" cartoon by W. C. Morris probably summarized the beliefs of League members fairly accurately. The League made effective use of cartoons in The Leader, *the party's principal newspaper. Most of the cartoons were drawn by John M. Baer, who served in the U.S. Congress from 1917 to 1921. Courtesy of the SHSND*

The opposition to the League regrouped and counter-attacked. The Independent Voters Association, or IVA, charged the League was socialist, unpatriotic, and un-American. Every action by League officials was attacked as contrary to established values, including the choice of books by the State Library Commission. Courtesy of the SHSND

cidents did occur and political opponents of the Nonpartisan League tried to paint it as disloyal to the American cause.

Although World War I greatly increased the demand for farm products, and the government urged farmers to plant all available land, the war did not bring great prosperity to North Dakota. Drought and poor crops limited production. The year 1917 was the driest year recorded since statehood; not until 1934 would the state experience so little rain again. The government regulated prices and set the price of wheat at two-thirds of what an unregulated price would have brought. Farm labor was scarce, and through it all land prices increased.

Although price controls and some relatively poor harvests had muted the prosperity of the wartime period, the good times had polished the dreams of many North Dakotans. Politically, the success of the NPL provided hope that farmers would be able to control their destiny, regulate those whom many North Dakotans saw as exploiters, and use state resources to market farm products and provide needed capital. In addition, the automobile was changing the countryside, removing some of the isolation caused by the distances which separated people, and increasing choices where people might shop or carry on their other activities. Increasing mechanization (and North Dakota agriculture was always at the forefront in mechanization) promised

greater productivity and relief from some of farming's drudgery.

As the reality of the postwar period set in, the bright dreams lost some of their luster. The Roaring Twenties provided uneven prosperity in the country. After a brief postwar depression, the U.S. economy boomed, fueled by sales from automobiles, radios, refrigerators, washing machines and the like. But the farm economy didn't boom and circumstances sometimes seemed to conspire against the North Dakota farm economy. In 1919, with wheat prices still at the relatively high price of $2.35 per bushel, drought conditions produced an extremely poor crop. Production recovered, but prices fell—to $1.01 per bushel in 1921. Land prices fell as well—dropping one-third in value between 1920 and 1925. Farmers drew on their savings and, for a time, increased their mortgage debt. All of this affected the state's banks. North Dakota had 898 banks in 1920, 3 for every incorporated place. Lax regulation led to instability, while an inadequately funded deposit-guarantee law had encouraged deposits. As the farm economy collapsed, the banks began to falter. By 1933, 573 of the 898 banks that had been in operation in 1920 were closed and depositors had lost fifty million dollars.

But if the 1920s brought hard times, the 1930s brought disaster. The state dried up. Of the eleven years from 1929 through 1939, only two had average or above average rainfall. One of those two years, 1935, was sandwiched between the two driest years in history. Added to the burden of drought was the plague of grasshoppers, a periodic menace to the state. Grasshoppers destroyed crops, ate canvases off of binders and clothes off of lines, cut binder twine on bundles of grain, and even chewed on fenceposts and pitchfork handles.

The Great Depression conspired with nature. A bushel of wheat, which brought $2.35 in 1919 and $1.01 in 1921, brought $.36 in 1932. The low farm income of the 1920s was cut in half during the 1930s even when government payments were included. At times nearly half the people in the state received government assistance. Although the entire nation suffered throughout the Depression, North Dakota hurt even more. Per capita personal income in North Dakota was less than one-half of the national average. Loans went delinquent, mortgages were foreclosed upon, taxes went unpaid.

People fled. After growing slowly during the 1920s (from 646,872 to 680,845), the state's population steadily declined during the 1930s, falling to 641,935 in 1940. The farm population, which grew a meager 8 percent during the 1920s, now plunged more than 17 percent.

By and large the state survived on a flood of federal money administered through a succession of alphabet soup agencies, starting with the Reconstruction Finance Corporation, then the Federal Emergency Relief Administration (FERA), the Civil Works Administration (CWA), and the Works Progress Administration (WPA). Of the thirty-six million dollars paid out in relief from 1933 through 1935, thirty-two million dollars was furnished by the federal government. These federal programs provided more than a dole, however. North Dakotans employed on CWA, FERA,

and WPA projects built streets, highways, bridge public buildings, dams, swimming pools, airports, and parks. They served school lunches, inventoried historical records, conducted research, produced pottery, and wrote a book o the state. These projects not only provided employment for thousands (in 1936 nearly sixty-one thousand people were employed und various programs), but also provided an important infrastructure of roads, bridges, and sewage treatment plants, which would be in place when prosperity returned.

The politics of the era were as turbulent as the economics. A recall election on October 28, 192 removed Gov. Lynn J. Frazier, Attorney General William Lemke, and Commissioner of Agricultu and Labor John N. Hagen, from office—Nonpart san League officials who had won at the polls le: than a year earlier. The following year Frazier wa elected to the United States Senate. Lemke was elected to Congress in 1932. North Dakota's political battles were carried on primarily within the Republican party, between Leaguers and Independents (Independent Voters Association or IVA), and at times between conservative and liberal Leaguers. Of the many political personali ties of the era, none was as popular, controversia or significant as William Langer. The former Morton County state's attorney, who had won a reputation by arresting bootleggers and successfully suing the Northern Pacific Railway Compan was elected attorney general under the Nonparti san League banner in 1916. Langer openly opposed League leadership in 1919, strongly attacking League organizer Arthur C. Townley an Governor Frazier. Unsuccessful in gaining the Republican nomination for governor in 1920, Langer reentered the League in 1928 and began to reshape it in his image. Elected governor in

Even though the League was defeated with the recall election of 1921, the State Mill and Elevator was constructed, and the Bank of North Dakota continued by an Industrial Commission controlled by the Independent Voters Association. Gov. Ragnvold A. Nestos promised to give the League's creations a fair trial. Both continue to exist. Courtesy of the SHSND

32, Langer took dramatic actions—a mora-
ium on foreclosures on March 4, 1933, and an
1bargo on all wheat shipments from the state in
e fall of that year—which raised morale and
ured Langer's reputation as a man of action.
1ger's other actions—political appointments
d solicitation of political contributions—also
oduced ammunition for his enemies. Convicted
soliciting and collecting money for political
1rposes from federal employees and of conspir-
g to obstruct the orderly operation of an act of
ongress, Langer was removed from office on
1y 17, 1934. After an appeal and three more
als, Langer was finally found innocent of all
arges late in 1935. In a three-way race the
lowing year, Langer was again elected governor
ith only 36 percent of the vote. Failing in his bid
unseat incumbent Sen. Gerald P. Nye in
38. Langer came back in 1940 and in another
ree-way race was elected to the United States
1nate with 38 percent of the vote. Overcoming
1 effort to prevent the Senate from seating him,
1nger retained his seat until his death late
1 1959.

During the 1920s and 1930s various attempts
ere made to address farmers' marketing prob-
ms. Cooperative elevators had been established
efore the turn of the century and had grown
gnificantly in number after 1900, numbering 264
1 1915, with more than a quarter of the state's
rmers as members of elevator associations. The
quity Cooperative Exchange was organized in
008 as a terminal marketing agency in Minnea-
olis. After a bitter and protracted struggle with
1e Minneapolis Chamber of Commerce, the Ex-
nange moved to St. Paul in 1914 and thereafter
xpanded rapidly. Poor management led to bank-
1ptcy in 1923. But the apparent success of the
xchange encouraged other cooperatives to form

and the Standard Marketing Act, passed by the
North Dakota Legislative Assembly in 1921,
legalized monopoly control of the market by
farmers' organizations. The Capper-Volstead Act,
passed by Congress in 1922, exempted agricultural cooperatives from the antitrust laws. An
attempt to secure a monopoly in the marketing of
hard spring wheat met with failure, however. The
North Dakota Wheat Growers Association, organized in 1922, faced the hostility of the grain trade
and coped with the growers' financial problems,
only to be forced out of business in 1930 by
losses in part attributable to the actions of the
Federal Farm Board.

The most conspicuously successful organization during this period was the North Dakota
Farmers' Union. The Farmers' Union Terminal
Association took over the Equity Cooperative
Exchange operations in 1926. In November 1927,
the North Dakota Farmers' Union was organized
with its headquarters at Jamestown. Within a year,
it was one of the two largest state units in the
National Farmers' Union.

The era between the two world wars was the
most difficult in the state's history. Coming on the
heels of a period of such great expansion, the
shock and the contrast were all the greater. The
fragile nature of the environment was exposed
again, as it had been to some extent when the
Slope had been overgrazed in the 1880s. But this
time the lesson could not be ignored. North
Dakotans became more aware of water problems,
establishing the State Water Conservation
Commission in 1937, passing the Water Conservation Districts Law in 1935, and cooperating with
federal agencies in programs for soil and water
conservation. Shelter belts were planted and
would become a prominent feature on the landscape. Trying times provide lessons for the future,

North Dakotans' interest in
automobiles was immediate.
At the turn of the century,
automobiles were a novelty
which stirred interest as they
first arrived. By early 1908,
when this photograph was
taken in front of the Martin
Jacobsen home in Minot,
autos were becoming much
more common. This group
had just completed a January
11 and 12 auto tour from
Bottineau to Minot. At least
one Dickinson land company
replaced their horse-drawn
buggies with a high-wheeled
steam automobile to tour their
clients. The number of autos
owned by North Dakotans
grew from 13,075 in 1913 to
92,000 in 1920. By 1915, the
Ford Model T was the base
upon which a new political
movement was organized—
the Nonpartisan League. Courtesy of the SHSND

In 1917, when this photograph was taken, the state had few graded roads and none were surfaced. Courtesy of the SHSND

Unfortunately, North Dakota's roads needed considerable improvement. During portions of each year, many of the state's roads could not be used. Courtesy of the SHSND

and North Dakotans learned caution and conservatism. Whether these lessons were the appropriate ones to take away from this era might be debated, but when a measure of prosperity returned, debts would be paid and savings put aside—principles which applied to individuals and government alike. But North Dakota remained principally an agricultural state and wheat remained king.

The Gillen Construction Company graveled a highway north of Harvey in 1922. The following year modern equipment was added to this job in the form of a 1923 Model T truck. By 1928, 2,400 miles of the state's 7,200 mile-long highway system had a gravel surface and 4,000 miles were graded.

Automobiles and improved roads changed North Dakota in many ways, removing isolation and aiding consolidation. Larger trading centers attracted customers from greater distances. Courtesy of the SHSND

The ferry operated on the Little Missouri River at Watford City by McKenzie County rancher William "Bill" Chaloner was representative of the primary method of crossing the state's rivers. Numerous bridges were built in the 1920s and 1930s, including such major structures as Liberty Memorial Bridge, dedicated at Bismarck on September 15, 1922, and Lewis and Clark Bridge, dedicated at Williston on July 1, 1927. Courtesy of the SHSND

The automobile transformed life in North Dakota even more than in other parts of the United States. In 1930 there was one automobile for every 5.3 persons in the country. In North Dakota the figure was one for every 3.7 persons. With increasing road mileage and numbers of cars, travelers' cabin courts became a fixture along the state's roads. This one was located at Jamestown. Courtesy of the SHSND

A State Highway Department snowplow accident was "caused by fog and steam off radiator," circa 1937-1938. More powerful and faster cars were produced in the 1930s and automobile accidents increased as well. In 1936, the state suffered 132 traffic deaths. The State Highway Patrol was created in 1935 to enforce the state's traffic laws—with a five-man force. Courtesy of the SHSND

This 1927 photo shows KGCU
radio station of Mandan. The
station later changed its call
letters to KBOM. The first
radio station was established
by Earl C. Reineke in Fargo.
WDAY received its license to
operate on May 22, 1922.
Reineke built his first radio
transmitter in Fargo in 1907
when he was thirteen years
old.

By 1930, six stations operated in North Dakota. Two,
KFYR in Bismarck and WDAY,
operated with one thousand-
watt transmitters. The other
four, KDLR (Devils Lake),
KPLM (Minot), KFJM (Grand
Forks), and KGCU, had one-
hundred-watt transmitters.
Courtesy of the SHSND

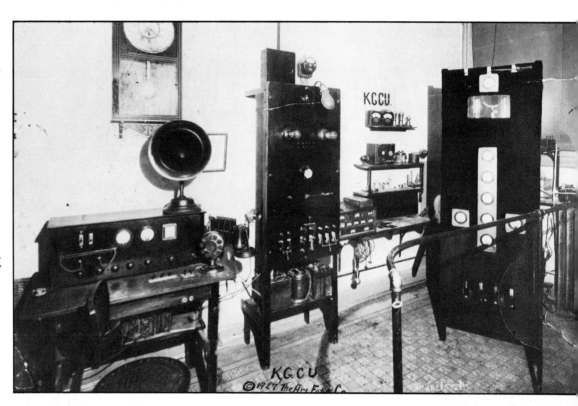

This quaint popcorn wagon
was a common sight in
Bismarck. Courtesy of the
SHSND

In an expedition led by Sir Hubert Wilkins, Hatton native Carl Ben Eielson made the first non-stop flight over the North Pole. Eielson, who enlisted in the Army Air Service in 1917, gained fame for his flying exploits in Alaska, including the first air mail service. While on a rescue mission off the north cape of Siberia in 1929, Eielson crashed. His body was brought out several months later. The whole state mourned with the ten thousand who assembled at the funeral in Hatton in March 1930. Eielson Air Force Base and a mountain in Alaska bear his name. Courtesy of the SHSND

Trinity Swedish Lutheran Church near Goose Lake in Logan County was photographed during a church anniversary celebration service in the early 1930s. As of 1936 a census of religious bodies showed that more than 41 percent of church members in North Dakota belonged to one of the Lutheran bodies, and almost 38 percent belonged to the Roman Catholic Church. The denomination with the next largest membership, with less than 5 percent of all North Dakota church members claiming affiliation, was the Methodist Episcopal Church, followed by Congregational and Christian churches, Presbyterians, and Baptists. Courtesy of the SHSND

President Franklin Roosevelt was greeted by an estimated thirty-five thousand people in Devils Lake on August 7, 1934. Devils Lake was the headquarters of the Missouri River Diversion Association and supporters of a project to divert the Missouri River's flood waters hoped to get the president's support. Instead, he promised to study the problem. "I expect to confer within the next few weeks with all the experts," the president said. "If it is possible for government to improve conditions in this state, government will do it." Other visits to North Dakota by President Roosevelt included Bismarck in 1936 and Grand Forks in 1937. Courtesy of the SHSND

While apparently overshadowed by the nearly 80 percent affiliation among church members with the Lutheran and Roman Catholic churches, other denominations have survived and flourished in the state. This Russian Baptist Conference meeting at Max about 1925 provides some indication of the diversity of traditions represented throughout North Dakota. Courtesy of the SHSND

The Second Baptist Church was located on South Eighth Street in Bismarck about 1920. Organized in 1917, this church had a membership of twelve in 1920. North Dakota's small black population grew steadily smaller, falling from 617 in 1910 to 467 in 1920 and 377 in 1930. Courtesy of the SHSND

As the 1920s progressed, the Washburn Lignite Coal Company experienced increasing problems. In 1928 the mines were sold to the Otter Tail Power Company and then leased by the Truax-Traer Company of Minot. The underground operations were closed and the mine converted to a large strip mine. Courtesy of the SHSND

Shown here in the early 1930s, this electrically-powered shovel of the Truax-Traer Company had a capacity of six yards of coal. The strip mining operation employed seventy miners when it went into full swing in August 1930. Five months earlier the underground operation which it replaced had employed 290 men. In 1922, four hundred men had been on the payroll. Courtesy of the SHSND

Roseglen State Bank was chartered in the fall of 1916 and was one of 898 banks operating in the state in 1920. The bank failed in 1926, one of 573 that went out of business between 1920 and 1933. It was also robbed twice during its ten-year existence. Courtesy of the SHSND

There was housing for the Truax-Traer Coal Company in the early 1930s. The mining operation was about eleven miles southwest of Velva. Courtesy of the SHSND

Taken in McHenry County on August 19, 1936, this photo shows the most extreme damage inflicted by drought and wind erosion during the period. The area had been overgrazed by sheep. With no vegetation to hold the light soil in place, the wind had removed from six to eight feet of soil. The original level of the soil is the top of the "island" where a few tufts of grass held the soil in place. U.S.D.A. Forest Service photo courtesy of the SHSND

Soil from an adjacent field drifted across a county road four miles north of Towner on May 9, 1936. The driest year recorded in North Dakota was 1936 with only 8.8 inches of precipitation. That surpassed the old record of 9.5 inches—set in 1934. U.S.D.A. Forest Service photo courtesy of the SHSND

Vast numbers of grasshoppers ate nearly everything in their path, including binder slats and canvases as well as crops. Cartoons joked that the grasshoppers used barbed wire to pick their teeth after they ate the fenceposts. Courtesy of the SHSND

Grasshoppers menaced the state throughout the 1930s. Farmers spread poison—arsenic mixed with various other materials—with spreaders such as these. Since the mixing was sometimes done by stirring the ingredients in such areas as barn floors, farmers undoubtedly inhaled a fair amount of the poison. Caches of leftover arsenic have been uncovered in recent years. Courtesy of the SHSND

This grasshopper net, near Willow City, was used in an effort to reduce the number of grasshoppers. Courtesy of the SHSND

Members of the Farm Holiday Association in Cass County gathered outside the home of a tenant farmer to prevent his eviction. Farm Holiday Association members used various tactics to prevent evictions, including the purchase of machinery for a few cents at foreclosure sales (and intimidating other prospective buyers), and returning the machinery to the original owner. Courtesy of the SHSND

This unidentified family posed in front of their dug-out home south of White Earth about 1930. For many, living conditions worsened throughout the period. Thousands fled the state and those who stayed "made do." Courtesy of the SHSND

North Dakota Farmers
[Uni]on was organized in
[Nov]ember 1927, with Charles
[T]albott as president and
[hea]dquarters in Jamestown.
[In 1]928 the organization had
[twe]nty thousand members in
[the] state, and by 1930 had
[org]anized locals in all but

eight counties. During the
1930s, the Farmers' Union
grew rapidly and exerted significant political power. This
photo was taken of the
Farmers Union Drought Relief
in Ward County, February
1931. Courtesy of the SHSND

[On] December 28, 1930, the
[sta]te capitol burned. Original-
[ly b]uilt as the capitol of
[D]akota Territory in 1883, the
[bu]ilding had been added to
[twi]ce. State offices found

space wherever available,
moving some offices into the
Liberty Memorial Building
and salvaging a portion of an
addition to the old capitol.
Courtesy of the SHSND

Pickets stand guard by the capitol construction site in May 1933. Common laborers walked off the job on May 16, demanding better working conditions and fifty cents an hour in wages rather than their existing pay of thirty cents an hour. Gov. William Langer ordered the general contractor to resume operations on May 24. Violence broke out when skilled laborers attempted to cross the picket line. On June 1 the governor imposed martial law and had National Guard troops stationed at the capitol construction site. The next day the strike ended and work resumed. Common laborers now received 40 cents an hour, mortar mixers fifty cents an hour, and the normal work week was to be forty-eight hours.

A bid by Jamestown to remove the capitol to that city had been turned down by North Dakota voters in 1932. The capitol was completed in 1934 at a cost of about $2 million. Courtesy of the SHSND

William and Lydia Langer and daughters posed for a family portrait. With her husband temporarily barred from seeking the office, Lydia Langer took his place as Republican candidate for governor in 1934. Courtesy of the SHSND

"We want Langer!" Crowds marched through the streets of Bismarck on July 19, 1934, demonstrating support for William Langer, who had been removed from office by the state supreme court, as Lt. Gov. Ole H. Olson moved into the governor's office. Courtesy of the SHSND

Ole H. Olson was sworn in as governor in July 1934. With Lydia Langer as the Republican candidate that fall, Olson and other old Leaguers supported the Democratic candidate, Thomas H. Moodie. Courtesy of the SHSND

Thomas H. Moodie, elected governor in 1934, had been a resident of North Dakota since 1898—except for a period from August 1929 to April 1931, when he worked in Minneapolis. Langer discovered that Moodie had voted in Minneapolis in 1930. On February 2, 1935, the state supreme court disqualified Moodie on the grounds that he did not meet the North Dakota constitutional provision of residing in the state for five years immediately preceding the election. Courtesy of the SHSND

Moodie's disqualification elevated Lt. Gov. Walter Welford, shown seated at his desk in the state capitol, North Dakota's fourth governor in seven months. Welford secured the Republican nomination in 1936, but along with Democratic candidate John Moses, lost to William Langer running as an Independent in the three-way race. Courtesy of the SHSND

This WPA crew leveling the street in Leith around 1938 was one of many in operation throughout North Dakota. In addition to providing relief, the WPA built 20,373 miles of highways and streets. Before that, the FERA had built more than 2,300 miles of streets and highways. Courtesy of the SHSND

The Tolley Community Hall was one of 503 new public buildings constructed by the WPA. The WPA also built sixty-one additions to public buildings. Courtesy of the SHSND

The Burlington Subsistence Homestead Project was intended to provide small irrigated plots to ease the plight of miners and their families. Courtesy of the SHSND

The Linton Sewage Treatment plant was one of thirty-nine such facilities constructed by the WPA. In addition, the WPA built nine water treatment plants and 809 water wells. Courtesy of the SHSND

Civil Works Administration funds purchased a lighting system for the Fargo airport, while FERA money built a new hangar and improved two runways and airport drainage. The WPA constructed a combined terminal and airport administration building in 1935 and 1936. This photo was taken in 1936. Courtesy of the SHSND

4-H Club girls plant a garden in a portion of the Indian Service Irrigated Garden at Fort Yates in the spring of 1939. State Water Conservation Commission photo courtesy of the SHSND

Edgar White, shown harvesting wheat east of Park River in 1937, left the stubble long as an erosion control measure. Such conservation practices were implemented as a result of the severe drought of the 1930s. The eastern part of the state suffered less from the drought conditions. This field produced between fifteen and twenty bushels to the acre according to the U.S. Department of Agriculture. The John Deere "D" tractor pulling the combine was an extremely popular model, being produced for more than thirty years beginning in 1923. Courtesy of the SHSND

High school girls from Carrington cultivated a shelterbelt on the property of Ida McCreary one-half mile east of Carrington in August 1939. In an effort to publicize and encourage the planting of shelterbelts or windbreaks, the U.S. Forest Service used photos such as these. Here, they noted, was a group of high school girls "enjoying their summer vacation, cultivating a windbreak." Courtesy of the SHSND

Where possible, there was an increasing use of irrigation. This irrigated alfalfa field was located in McKenzie County in 1938. State Water Conservation Commission photo courtesy of the SHSND

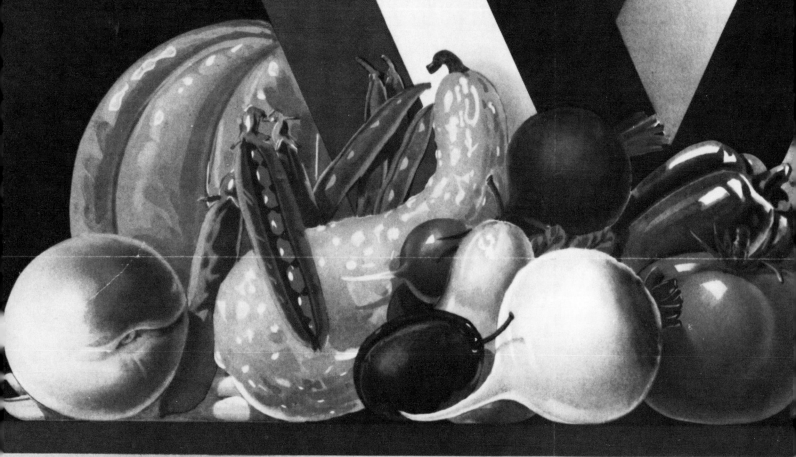

GROW YOUR

Be su

GARDEN

V IN 1945

FOR VICTORY

6

WAR YEARS AND NEW PROSPERITY THE 1940S AND 1950S

North Dakotans were still reeling from the effects of the Great Depression when war came to our shores in 1941. In addition to a global economic depression in the 1930s, many areas of the world witnessed the rise of dictators and suffered from war: civil war in Spain, Japan warring against China, the Italo-Ethiopian War, and the rearming of Germany. Most Americans deplored war and were determined to avoid any military involvement. Isolationism was a long-standing American tradition.

North Dakotans especially embodied the isolationist spirit. U.S. Sen. Gerald P. Nye of North Dakota, like many Americans, was convinced munitions manufacturers and financiers led the United States into the Great War to ensure the Allied victory that was necessary to protect wartime investments and credit to those countries. In 1934, Senator Nye was named chairman of a Senate committee to investigate the manufacture and sale of munitions to the Allied belligerents during World War I. The committee's findings supported the idea that economic forces—not a direct military threat to the United States—caused our entry into World War I. Gut reactions to the horrors of the war and the findings of the "Nye Committee" caused a resurgence of American isolationism. The activities of the Senate investigation lasted until 1937. For a time, this exposure made Gerald Nye a household word in America.

These revelations concerning American entry into World War I contributed to enactment of neutrality laws prohibiting American aid to nations at war. When general war broke out in Europe in 1939, there was little the Roosevelt Administration could do about it. Most Americans opposed aid to nations battling Hitler and Mussolini; many flocked to the America First Committee, an organization dedicated to keeping the United States out of war. Senator Nye was a prominent supporter and speaker for the America First Committee, as were other well-known Americans, such as Charles A. Lindbergh. The entire North Dakota Congressional delegation supported the neutrality acts and American isolationism. Most North Dakotans, like most Americans, adopted a pre-1917 mentality concerning the war raging in Europe. Even after Norway, the Low Countries, and France fell in 1940, few were diverted from their isolationist stance.

The Japanese attack on Pearl Harbor on December 7, 1941, changed everything. North Dakotans, like virtually all Americans, dropped isolationism and ardently waged war against the enemies of the United States. Even though North

This store window in the Beulah/Hazen area contains photographs of men and women serving in the armed forces of the United States during World War II. Communities took pride in the young people from their area serving in the armed forces. Over seventy thousand North Dakotans served in World War II; 1,995 were killed. Courtesy of the SHSND

This political cartoon pictures North Dakota Sen. Gerald P. Nye encountering Senate criticism for the activities and findings of the "Nye Committee." The "Nye Committee" investigated the alleged connection between the munitions manufacturers and financiers and American entry into World War I. The publicity resulting from the activities of the "Nye Committee" made Gerald Nye a household word in America during the 1930s. Gerald Nye was defeated in the 1944 Senate election by Gov. John Moses. Courtesy of the SHSND

Gasoline rationing was a fact of life in wartime North Dakota. Gasoline ration coupon books, like the one pictured here, were in use in North Dakota during World War II. Careful management of mileage and coupons was necessary to ensure that enough gas could be purchased for a motorist to get around. Courtesy of the SHSND

Shown here is the launching of the U.S.S. Grand Forks *at the Richmond Shipyard in California. Money for the U.S.S.* Grand Forks *was raised through subscription by the citizens of Grand Forks. The* Grand Forks *was christened by Inga Thoreson on November 27, 1943. Courtesy of the SHSND*

North Dakota flying ace Capt. Richard V. Grace is pictured here at the controls of a B-17 bomber in 1945. Growing up in Mohall, Grace was a flyer in World War I and later gained notoriety for his exploits as a Hollywood stunt flyer, airplane crasher, and wing walker. Grace flew numerous bombing missions over Germany. Courtesy of the SHSND

Fred G. Aandahl was the Republican governor of North Dakota from 1945 to 1950. Aandahl was a popular governor. A farmer from Litchville and a creator of the Republican Organizing Committee (ROC) in 1943, Aandahl was not able to defeat William Langer in the 1952 Senate race. The ROC was a coalition movement of Republicans and Leaguers united to oppose William Langer's control of the NPL. Courtesy of the SHSND

John Moses, the bespectacled man on the right with the sheep, was the Democratic governor of North Dakota from 1939 to 1945. Moses was a big man sporting enormously bushy eyebrows. A native of Norway, John Moses was elected to the United States Senate in 1944, but died soon after taking the oath of office in 1945. Courtesy of the SHSND

This jolly German seaman served for a while as an internee at the internment camp at Fort Lincoln, Bismarck, during World War II. More than two thousand German and Japanese nationals spent time at Fort Lincoln during the war. At least seven internees escaped, though all were eventually captured. Courtesy of the SHSND

akota had one of the highest rates of agricultural deferments, over 70,000 North Dakotans served with the armed forces of the United States. The North Dakota National Guard was federalized. North Dakotans served in every theatre of the war and 1,995 were called to make the supreme sacrifice.

In addition to military service, North Dakotans contributed to the war effort by buying $397 million in war bonds. Others helped by collecting paper, scrap metal, old tires, and fats for war industries. The colleges and universities served as military training centers, and Fort Lincoln in Bismarck was converted to an internment camp where enemy aliens were incarcerated.

Rationing of many foodstuffs and products, such as tires and gasoline, was a fact of life for wartime America. Despite the shortages imposed by war rationing, a measure of prosperity returned to North Dakota. Abundant rain and rising agricultural commodity prices made farming profitable once again. By February 1943, all of the New Deal relief programs were gone. North Dakota did not, however, join in the prosperity resulting from construction of defense plants and profitable wartime industry contracts. Virtually no defense industries spawned or were relocated in North Dakota. Thousands left North Dakota during the war to take jobs in defense plants elsewhere.

Another war, also heavily opposed by North Dakotans, followed on the heels of World War II. Beginning in 1950, the Korean War involved 5,322 North Dakotans; 197 were killed. State leaders opposed the war; the state legislature called for evacuation of American troops from Korea, and Gov. C. Norman Brunsdale wanted to have army recruiters withdrawn from North Dakota. Despite the opposition, North Dakotans still contributed to the war effort.

During the 1940s and 1950s, North Dakotans worked to overcome the obstacles of remoteness and isolation that have historically stunted the economic and social growth of the state. Considerable resources were devoted to improvement of transportation and communication systems, upgrading the quality of life in the form of creature comforts and conveniences in rural areas, extension of electrical and telephone services to rural areas, diversification of agricultural output, and exploitation of mineral resources, especially oil and lignite coal.

The years following the war were good ones for agriculture. Farmers during and after the war reduced their indebtedness and expanded land holdings. Farm tenancy decreased and personal income increased. Greater emphasis was placed in the 1950s on soil conservation, with numerous soil conservation districts located throughout the state. Great farm surpluses developed and new federal farm programs offered greater price supports for agricultural commodities and took land out of production and reserved it in "soil banks." Average farm size and land values increased, reflecting a continuing trend to exten-

Mandan is famous for its annual Independence Day rodeo. Embodying a kinship for ranch life, many North Dakotans are avid rodeo fans. Marjorie Greenough rides "Buster" at the 1941 Mandan Rodeo. Female bronco busters in the 1940s were somewhat of a rarity. Courtesy of the SHSND

sive, specialized, and mechanical operations. Diversification of agricultural production also made way in the 1950s with growth in cultivation of sugar beets, barley, soybeans, and raising of beef cattle. Despite diversification, wheat was still king.

State population shifted dramatically after World War II, dropping to 619,000 in 1950. Many people left due to unemployment or farm foreclosure. The urban population grew while the rural population fell, causing the decline of many small communities in North Dakota.

Life changed for North Dakotans in other ways. In 1935, only 2.3 percent of North Dakota farms had electrical power. Rural electrification continued to spread rapidly, especially after World War II. Electrical and telephone cooperatives flourished. Rural Electrification Administration loans peaked in 1949 and by 1954 some 90 percent of all farms had electricity. By 1960, thirty-six thousand farms received telephone service.

School consolidation was spurred on by a 1947 law facilitating the process. By 1961, there were about 33 percent fewer school districts and 60 percent fewer one-room schools than a decade before. A state foundation aid to schools system was inaugurated in 1959, and teacher certification requirements were more rigid. Better roads, state aid for school transportation, and an abundance of automobiles facilitated these changes. Other institutions, such as churches and social organizations, also consolidated or closed. North Dakotans

Milton R. Young was appointed to the United States Senate by Gov. Fred Aandahl following the death of Sen. John Moses in 1945. A farmer from Berlin and veteran of the state House and Senate, Milton Young served in the U.S. Senate until 1981, serving longer than any other North Dakotan. Courtesy of the SHSND

*Sen. Milton Young, Congress-
man Otto Krueger, Clyde
Duffy, and C. Norman Brunsdale are pictured here. Born
in the Ukraine, Otto Krueger
was the first German-Russian
sent to Washington by North
Dakota. A Republican, Krueger
served first as state Insurance
Commissioner and later in the
U.S. House of Representatives
from 1953 to 1959. Courtesy
of the SHSND*

*Orin G. Libby reorganized the
State Historical Society of
North Dakota in 1905 and
served as its secretary until
1945. Known as the "Father
of North Dakota history,"
Libby was a longtime history
professor at the University of
North Dakota. Courtesy of the
SHSND*

tended to resist these changes because the loss of
schools and other organizations contributed to
the decline of small towns and rural areas.

Federally-funded programs reinvigorated the
North Dakota economy. Construction of Garrison
Dam on the upper Missouri River between 1946
and 1953 brought millions of federal dollars and
hundreds of jobs to the state, and provided a
means for hydroelectric production as well as
flood control downstream. Garrison Dam, mea-
suring half a mile thick at the base, sixty feet at the
summit, and more than two miles long, was
completed in 1953 with President Dwight Eisenhower attending the closure ceremonies. The
reservoir behind the dam, Lake Sakakawea, provides a recreational outlet for many North
Dakotans and a source of tourist revenue. An
enormous hydroelectric power station was completed in 1956. "Power on the line" was the
slogan marking inauguration of hydroelectric
power generation in North Dakota.

A tragic consequence of the Garrison Dam was
the flooding of some 150,000 acres of the Fort
Berthold Indian Reservation. Much of the land
was prime riverbottom of great value to the
Indians. A number of towns on the reservation,
and hundreds of Indians and whites were
uprooted and relocated elsewhere on the
reservation.

The original Pick-Sloan Plan of 1944 creating
the Garrison Dam included a plan to divert Souris
and Missouri river waters for irrigation in North
Dakota. The Missouri-Souris Diversion Unit, as the
plan was called, was fraught with problems from
the start. Initially, the Crosby-Mohall area to be
irrigated was later determined to be unsuitable
for irrigation. The plan was revised and renamed

Long the largest city in North Dakota, Fargo in the early 1940s boasted of six motion picture houses, thirty hotels, a golf course at Edgewood Park, a city bus and taxi service, and Hector Field. Note the tracks for the street railway. Courtesy of the SHSND

he Garrison Diversion Unit in 1957. This plan called for construction of canals to divert water from Garrison Reservoir to irrigate lands in central North Dakota. Approximately 6,773 miles of main and lateral canals, eight reservoirs, water supply for forty-one towns, and 9,300 miles of drains were proposed at a projected cost of $529 million (1956 prices). The project would take up to sixty years to complete. Congress balked at the amount, length of time for the project, and the poor estimated return on the investment. It was expected returns on hydroelectric power generation would help pay for the project. Congress appropriated funds for a much smaller project in 1965. Controversy over the need for the Garrison Diversion Unit continues to dog supporters of the project today.

Other monumental federal projects in North Dakota during the 1950s included construction of the Minot and Grand Forks Air Force bases. Both Minot and Grand Forks enthusiastically welcomed the air bases and labored to assist in their location in North Dakota. Construction began in 1956 and continued through 1957. Both bases were operational by the early 1960s. Strategic Air Command bombers and support aircraft were located at both bases, thus putting North Dakota at the forefront of America's nuclear strike and defense capability. In 1963, the first Minuteman Intercontinental Ballistic Missile silos were erected and readied for deployment. Today, some three hundred silos in North Dakota help protect the United States from nuclear attack.

Work began on North Dakota's part of the interstate highway system soon after enactment of the federal Interstate Highway System Act in 1956. By 1964, 242 of North Dakota's allotted 570 miles

were completed. The interstate highway system was a great economic benefit to the state and did much to link North Dakotans with the rest of the nation. Transportation increasingly shifted to the highways, though railroads were still the primary transportation for goods.

The Theodore Roosevelt National Memorial Park was created from a state park in the Badlands in 1948. Two units, one near Medora and one further north near the site of Roosevelt's Elkhorn Ranch, are under supervision of the National Park Service. A tribute to Roosevelt and his years in North Dakota, the park is a major wildlife refuge, as well as a scenic tourist attraction.

Energy development got off to a jump start when the Amerada Oil Company discovered oil near Tioga on the Clarence Iverson farm in 1951. Oil came from the Nesson Anticline, part of the Williston Basin in eastern Montana, western North Dakota, northern South Dakota, and southern Canada. Discovery set off an oil boom in the western part of the state with oil production centered in Williams, McKenzie, Mountrail, Billings, Bottineau, and Burke counties. Thousands flocked to western North Dakota to search for oil and jobs. A 1954 booklet entitled, *Williston, Where Wheat Grows and Oil Flows*, reflected the enthusiasm and high hopes for oil production in that area. Local services and housing were initially exhausted. By the late 1960s, over twenty-five million barrels of oil were produced from more than two thousand wells. Standard Oil built a pipeline from Tioga to Mandan and a refinery at the Mandan terminus. Later, a refinery was constructed at Williston and natural gas processing plants at McGregor, Lignite, and Tioga. Oil production was a major diversification of the state's

Main streets all across North Dakota are lighted and decorated in celebration of Christmas. This photo of Fargo was taken during the holiday season in the 1940s. Courtesy of the SHSND

In 1955, Jamestown had a population of 14,200; two banks; twenty-one churches; four parks; six manufacturing establishments producing, among other things, milk products, soft drinks, and meat packing products; one newspaper; six hotels; two railroads, including the home office of the Midland Continental Railroad; two radio stations; two motion-picture theatres; and three hospitals. Jamestown has been the home of the North Dakota State Hospital since 1885 and the headquarters of the North Dakota Farmers' Union. Courtesy of the SHSND

economy and caused much change in areas of western North Dakota.

Coal mining also increased during the 1950s with construction of coal-fired electrical generating plants at Mandan and Velva in 1952 and 1954. Strip mining replaced deep mining as the means of extracting coal in the state.

Other developments worked to bring North Dakotans closer to the nation and closer together. The first television station, KCJB-TV Minot, went on the air on Easter Sunday 1953. WDAY-TV Fargo and KFYR-TV Bismarck followed suit later the same year. The number of radio stations increased while the number of newspapers continued to decline.

During the 1940s and 1950s, North Dakota farmers remained well organized. In addition to the North Dakota Farmers' Union, reorganized in 1927, the North Dakota Farm Bureau was created in 1942. With membership concentrated in the eastern half of the state, the Farm Bureau is more conservative, stressing personal initiative, the free enterprise system, and less government aid to agriculture. The Farm Bureau was often allied with the Greater North Dakota Association, the state chamber of commerce. In contrast, the

Farmers' Union dominates the west, is more liberal, favors protection of family farms, supports organized labor, and manages extensive cooperative business interests, such as the Farmers Union Central Exchange (later known as CENEX) and the Grain Terminal Association (GTA). Both organizations maintained insurance companies (Farmers' Union insurance companies and NoDak Mutual), and both organizations played important roles in state politics from the 1940s to the present.

In politics and government, North Dakota witnessed change during the 1940s and the 1950s. The state experienced formation of a two-party political system, and some reform and expansion in the organization and role of state government. Politically, the 1940s opened with Democrat (though not a New Dealer) John Moses in the governor's chair, and the Republican party divided between a Nonpartisan League closely linked with William Langer and an amorphous opposition coalition. A conservative group within the Republican party led by Fred Aandahl, Milton Young, and others, created the Republican Organizing Committee (ROC) in 1943. The ROC sought to create a unified and conservative Republican party by purging the party of Langer Republicans and the more liberal elements of the Nonpartisan League. The ROC successfully elected Fred Aandahl as governor and acquired majorities in the state House and Senate in 1944. Gov. John Moses was elected to the U.S. Senate, but died soon after assuming office. Governor Aandahl appointed Milton Young to fill Moses's empty seat.

After the 1944 elections, the ROC became the dominant political force in the state. Aandahl won reelection as governor in 1946, and Milton Young was victorious in his bid for the U.S. Senate seat in a special election. Despite these successes, the ROC was unable to upset William Langer in the 1946 primary; Langer returned to the U.S. Senate in the fall.

The 1947 legislature, controlled by the ROC, attempted to damage the North Dakota Farmers' Union by enacting legislation limiting their insurance program and taxing the surplus earnings of its cooperatives. Though the legislation failed to pass, the confrontation brought the Farmers' Union into the political arena to stay. Reflecting a conservative, anti-union attitude, the Legislative Assembly successfully enacted a law making North Dakota a "right to work" state in 1947.

In June 1947, the Farmers' Union created the Farmers' Union Progressive Alliance. In cooperation with organized labor and the Nonpartisan League, the Farmers' Union Progressive Alliance formed the Committee for Progressive Unity in 1948. At the Nonpartisan League state convention in 1948, a slate of candidates was endorsed that represented the Committee for Progressive Unity. The NPL elected Usher Burdick to the House, landed a few state offices, and gained a majority

The years following WW II were good ones for agriculture. Abundant precipitation during and after the war provided good yields. Farmers were able to reduce their indebtedness and expand their land holdings. Great farm surpluses developed in the 1950s. New federal government farm programs offered greater price supports for agricultural commodities and took land out of production and reserved it in "soil banks." Average farm size and land values increased, reflecting a trend toward extensive, specialized, and mechanical operations. Despite some gains in agricultural diversification, wheat was still king in North Dakota. Courtesy of the SHSND

Due to the chronic shortage of teachers, Roman Catholic nuns often taught in public schools; by 1947, seventy-four sisters were teaching in public schools. In 1948, an initiated measure prohibiting teachers from wearing religious garb in public schools passed by 93,469 to 83,038. The measure was supported by Protestant and Masonic organizations and opposed by the Catholic Church. After the anti-garb measure became law, sisters abandoned their habits and continued to teach in public schools. Courtesy of the Diocese of Bismarck archives

Kitchen and food servers posed at the Williams County Farmers' Union cooperative cafeteria, Williston, in 1949. A local of the North Dakota Farmers' Union, the Williams County Farmers' Union was and still is the largest and most active local in the state. By the late 1940s, the Williams County Farmers' Union helped establish a wide variety of cooperatives to provide goods and services to farmers and their families throughout Williams County. Cooperative ventures included electric co-ops, elevators, stores, a cafeteria, an oil company, credit unions, groceries, creameries, a lumberyard and a hospital. Courtesy of the SHSND

In 1944, the Pick-Sloan Plan for managing the waters of the Missouri River Basin called for construction of one of the projects' dams across the Missouri in North Dakota. Construction of Garrison Dam began in 1947. Closure of the dam was made in 1953, with earthwork completed in 1954. The project cost approximately $294 million. This 1950 photo shows a giant Euclid earth mover being loaded to haul away soil for construction of the Garrison Dam. Courtesy of the SHSND

in the state House. ROC supporters returned Fred Aandahl to the governor's office.

By the 1950s, the Nonpartisan League was roughly split into two factions, the liberals or the "insurgents," and the conservatives or the "old guard." The "old guard" leaned toward the Republican party and the "insurgents" were more in line with the Democratic party. The ROC and the "insurgents" wanted a party realignment with the "old guard" joining the Republicans and the Nonpartisan League merging with the Democratic party. The Farmers' Union was leaning toward the Democratic party by the early 1950s. The ROC returned Milton Young to the Senate in 1950, but Fred Aandahl failed in an attempt to beat William Langer out of the Senate in 1952. C. Norman Brunsdale was elected to the first of two terms as governor.

The long-awaited realignment occurred in 1956. At the Nonpartisan League state convention the delegates voted to run their candidates in the Democratic column. The Democratic state convention voted to endorse the NPL candidates and adopted its platform. Later the ROC welcomed the "old guard" faction at their state convention. For the first time in North Dakota history, a two-party system was in place. Despite the merger of the Democratic-NPL parties, the ROC was still successful in 1956 with John Davis winning the governor's chair and Milton Young returning to the U.S. Senate. Old-time Leaguers William Langer and Usher Burdick stayed with the Republican party in spite of the realignment.

Though the Democratic-NPL party was less powerful than the Republican party, it began to grow in numbers and successes. In 1958, the Democratic-NPL party was able to send Quentin Burdick, son of Usher Burdick, to the U.S. House of Representatives. Thus, for the first time in history, a Democrat from North Dakota sat in the House of Representatives. Despite this success,

The city of Riverdale was established to house the thousands of workers who labored for years to complete the Garrison Dam. Employment peaked in 1952, with twenty-three hundred workers on the dam project. Riverdale was owned by the federal government until it incorporated in 1987. Courtesy of the SHSND

e ROC was still in control of the state government with the reelection of John Davis to the governorship. The election of Democratic-NPL candidate William Guy as governor in 1960 ended sixteen years of ROC hegemony and signaled the completion of the two-party system in North Dakota.

The 1950s closed with the retirement or death of a number of longtime and notable political figures: William Lemke died in 1950; William Langer and Arthur C. Townley died within a few days of each other in 1959; Usher Burdick retired in 1959, as did State Auditor Berta Baker, North Dakota's most successful woman politician, in 1957.

The state government experienced expansion and some reorganization during the 1940s and '50s. A Governmental Survey Commission was created in 1941 to study and make recommendations on improvement of the structure and functions of state government. The report made many recommendations; very few were implemented immediately. A Legislative Research Committee was created in 1945 to assist the legislature in researching and crafting legislation. In recognition of the importance of economic growth for the state's future, the Legislative Assembly created the Economic Development Commission in 1957. A state agency, the role of the commission was to attract and facilitate economic development in North Dakota. State purchasing and accounting were centralized in a new state agency in 1959, the Department of Accounts and Purchases.

North Dakota experienced much change during the 1940s and 1950s. Of particular importance was modernization and lessening of the isolation and remoteness. In a sense, North Dakota "caught up" with the rest of the nation during this period. Increasing modernization and diversification continued and accelerated in the decades that followed.

This June 1959 aerial shows the spillway on the east end of the Garrison Dam. The city of Riverdale is in the right background, and to the left, a portion of the growing reservoir, Lake Sakakawea. Garrison is one of six dams in the Pick-Sloan Plan for development of the Missouri River Basin.

The Army Corps of Engineers manages Lake Sakakawea for flood control, generation of hydroelectric power, navigation, and irrigation. It also provides improved public water supplies, recreation, and fish and wildlife enhancement. Courtesy of the SHSND

171

In addition to flood control and a source of water supply, the Garrison Dam would host a hydroelectric power facility. Here the foundations for the power house and surge intakes are pictured in 1952. Seventy million yards of earth had to be moved to build the dam. Some 1.5 million yards of concrete were used in the Garrison Dam project. Courtesy of the SHSND

This is the control bay interior in the Garrison Dam power house, December 1955. Operators control every phase of the power plant's operation. In January 1956, the first of the plant's eighty-thousand kilowatt generators went into service and the fifth and final generator became operational in October 1960. Courtesy of the SHSND

Gov. C. Norman Brunsdale crowns a North Dakota Dairy Princess during the 1950s. A Republican, Brunsdale served as governor from 1951 to 1957. In 1959, Gov. John Davis appointed Brunsdale to the U.S. Senate to fill the vacancy caused by the death of William Langer. Brunsdale served in the Senate until 1960. Courtesy of the SHSND

Newscaster Bob MacLeod presents the intricacies of a new television camera to Bismarck viewers as KFYR-TV goes on the air in 1953. In the same broadcast, Meyer Broadcasting Company owner Etta Meyer spoke hopefully of the new medium "in which so much can be done, things never before possible." Courtesy of the SHSND

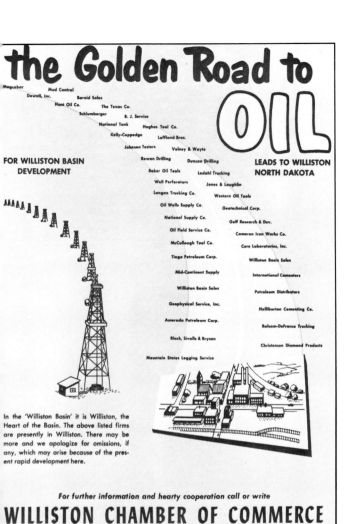

the Golden Road to OIL

Magcobar
Mud Control
Dowell, Inc.
Baroid Sales
Hunt Oil Co.
The Texas Co.
Schlumberger
B. J. Service
National Tank
Hughes Tool Co.
Kelly-Coppedge
Loffland Bros.
Johnson Testers
Volney & Wayte
Rowan Drilling
Duncan Drilling
Baker Oil Tools
Ledahl Trucking
Well Perforators
Jones & Laughlin
Langan Trucking Co.
Western Oil Tools
Oil Wells Supply Co.
Geotechnical Corp.
National Supply Co.
Gulf Research & Dev.
Oil Field Service Co.
Cameron Iron Works Co.
McCullough Tool Co.
Core Laboratories, Inc.
Tioga Petroleum Corp.
Williston Basin Sales
Mid-Continent Supply
International Cementers
Williston Basin Sales
Petroleum Distributers
Geophysical Service, Inc.
Halliburton Cementing Co.
Amerada Petroleum Corp.
Balsam-DeFrance Trucking
Black, Sivalls & Bryson
Christenson Diamond Products
Mountain States Logging Service

FOR WILLISTON BASIN DEVELOPMENT

LEADS TO WILLISTON NORTH DAKOTA

In the 'Williston Basin' it is Williston, the Heart of the Basin. The above listed firms are presently in Williston. There may be more and we apologize for omissions, if any, which may arise because of the present rapid development here.

For further information and hearty cooperation call or write

WILLISTON CHAMBER OF COMMERCE
WILLISTON, NORTH DAKOTA

...illiston welcomed the advent of the oil industry in the 1950s. Many ...companies and new businesses seemingly sprang up over night. ...is Chamber of Commerce publication proclaims "the golden road ...oil leads to Williston." Many of the businesses that sprang up and ...ospered during the oil boom are listed. Courtesy of the SHSND

NEWSMAN'S OIL TOUR GUEST

Oct. 4-5, 1957

Oil was discovered at Tioga by the Amerada Oil Company on the Clarence Iverson farm in 1951. Oil exploration and production boomed in Williston through the 1950s. This button recalls a special newsman's oil tour held by the Williston Chamber of Commerce. Courtesy of the SHSND

Shown here is the recently completed Amoco Oil Refinery in Mandan, Christmas night 1954. Standard Oil built a pipeline from Tioga to the refinery at Mandan. Later, a refinery was built at Williston. Courtesy of the SHSND

Ben Meier, a Republican from Napoleon, was first elected as North Dakota's secretary of state in 1954. Still in that position today, Ben Meier has been the secretary of state longer than any other state secretary in United States' history. Courtesy of the SHSND

John Dalager of Valley City bags an antelope south of Sentinel Butte in the 1950s. Historically, hunting has been a major recreation and industry for North Dakota. Courtesy of the SHSND

Appointed U.S. District Judge of Fargo in 1955, Ronald N. Davies made history when temporarily assigned to the federal bench in Little Rock, Arkansas. In 1957, Judge Davies rendered a landmark legal decision in racial integration when he ordered the Little Rock School Board to proceed with integration of Central High School, despite interference from Arkansas Gov. Orval Faubus. The effect of the decision was to deny pleas to hold off integration. The result was that President Eisenhower ordered federal troops into the area to preserve order and force integration of the high school. Courtesy of the SHSND

North Dakota high school students were photographed receiving driver training in 1958. Because of the vast distances and improving road surfaces, North Dakotans have been big on car ownership. From 1945 to 1960, the number of registered automobiles in the state increased 90 percent. By 1960, North Dakota had one car for each 1.8 persons, compared to one for each 2.5 persons nationally. Courtesy of the SHSND

By 1955, Bismarck had a population of 25,500; twenty-two churches; one daily, one semiweekly, and one weekly newspaper; two radio stations; ten hotels; twelve parks; 10,343 telephones; a symphony orchestra, concert choir, bands, Little Theatre, Light Opera Guild, and a Civic Music Association. This photo was taken of Bismarck during the Christmas season in the 1950s. Courtesy of the SHSND

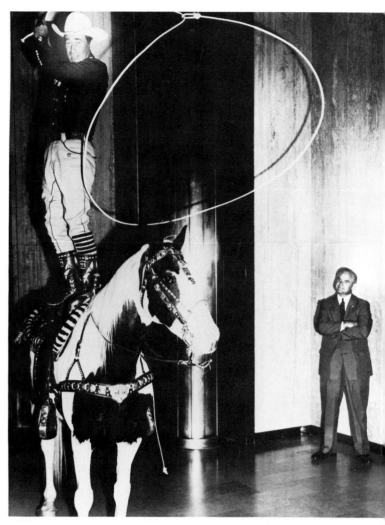

Gov. John E. Davis is enter-tained by Monty Montana and his horse Rex in the Great Hall of the State Capitol on July 2, 1958. A Republican, banker, and farmer/rancher from McClusky, John Davis was governor of North Dakota from 1957 to 1961. Davis ran for the U.S. Senate in 1960, but was defeated by Democrat Quentin Burdick. Davis was decorated in World War II, served as national com-mander of the American Legion in the mid-1960s, and was the director of the federal Civil Defense Agency from 1969 to 1977. Courtesy of the SHSND

This grand opening of a stretch of I-94 near James-town occurred in 1958. By 1964, 242 miles of North Dakota's interstate highway system was complete. Courtesy of the SHSND

The comely vamp pictured here is Molly Malloy, a character from "The Front Page," portrayed by actress Dorothy Stickney. A native of Dickinson, Dorothy Stickney achieved fame in the 1940s and 1950s in the Broadway hits "Life with Father," "Life with Mother," and "A Lovely Night." Courtesy of the SHSND

Aloisius Cardinal Muench, Bishop of Fargo, served as an intermediary between the United States Army and the Catholic hierarchy, and later was a representative of Pope Pius XII. He was appointed Papal Pro-Nuncio to the Federal Republic of Germany in 1951. Pope John XXIII elevated Bishop Muench to the College of Cardinals in 1959, thus making Aloisius Muench the only North Dakotan to be named a cardinal. Courtesy of the SHSND

Longtime State Auditor Berta E. Baker was the most successful woman to hold a state-wide office in North Dakota history. Berta Baker was state auditor from 1935 to 1957. Courtesy of the SHSND

181

One of the worst tornados in North Dakota history struck Fargo the evening of June 30, 1957. Running from the western part of the city to the north, the tornado ripped a swath three blocks wide. Sixty people were injured and ten killed. The tornado devastated a large portion of the city resulting in some ten million dollars worth of damage. A daring WDAY-TV cameraman filmed the tornado as it descended upon the city. This scene is from a television image called a kinescope. Courtesy of the SHSND

This is how the "Hasty Tasty" lunch counter appeared in the aftermath of the Fargo tornado, June 30, 1957. Courtesy of the SHSND

These slot machines were seized in raids on illegal gambling operations in Dickinson and Mandan in 1958. Twenty years later, North Dakotans would approve laws allowing some types of charitable casino-type gambling in hotels/motels, nightclubs, and service organizations. Courtesy of the SHSND

In 1958 Carpenters Local Union 1091 members waged a strike against the contractor building the McCabe Methodist Church in Bismarck. The labor movement has been relatively small throughout North Dakota history. Union membership surged to about eighteen thousand by the mid-1970s, but has been in decline in recent times. Courtesy of the SHSND

Douglas Wahl, senior sousaphone player, and Kathy Docktor, head majorette for the Bismarck High School Band, make eyes as well as music. The quality of high school education in North Dakota improved during the 1940s and 1950s. Small and numerous high schools in rural areas with few resources often robbed young North Dakotans of the quality education they deserved. The number of high schools declined from 433 in 1946 to 352 in 1960 due to school district consolidations, better application of slim resources, and better teachers. Courtesy of the SHSND

Reflecting the prevailing taste in rock and roll music among American youth, rock and roll bands proliferated in the 1950s through to the present. More traditional music in North Dakota, such as the polka, diminished in interest and currency. Courtesy of the SHSND

7

MODERN NORTH DAKOTA 1960 TO THE PRESENT

North Dakotans entered the 1960s with renewed hope for the future. Memories of the Great Depression and the struggle of World War II and Korea were dimming. Though the state supported Richard Nixon over John F. Kennedy in the 1960 presidential contest, North Dakotans seemed to be looking forward to the "New Frontier" of the future. Much growth and many changes occurred during the years of the 1960s to the centennial year of 1989.

Economically the 1960s through the 1980s witnessed years of prosperity, change, and increasing federal support for agriculture. Farm income doubled by 1969. More income came from non-farm sector sources, such as energy development, agricultural processing, and manufacturing. Personal income and state tax collections, due to oil and coal tax revenues, increased. Despite the increase in the non-agricultural sector over the years, agriculture still remains, overwhelmingly, the number one North Dakota industry in the 1980s. Agriculture became more dependent on federal support, comprising only 6 percent of farm income in 1960 and jumping to 18 percent by 1970. Agriculture continued to expand and diversify, though wheat was still king. Wheat acreage grew 12 percent and yields increased by one-third. Wheat remained, as ever, the largest cash crop in North Dakota.

Farms continued to consolidate and expand using larger and more sophisticated and expensive equipment. By 1980, the average farm was over 1,000 acres; in 1987 the average size farm was over 1,200 acres. The number of farms continued to decline: approximately 55,000 in 1960, 44,000 in 1970, 36,000 in 1980, and 33,000 today.

Agricultural production changed, reflecting a greater market orientation. Thus newer crops, such as dry edible beans, honey, sunflowers, and sugar beets were being produced in ever greater volume. Numbers of beef cattle increased, while numbers of milk cows and chickens declined. Agricultural processing industries expanded with sugar beet plants in the Red River Valley and sunflower processing plants also in the east.

Agricultural change was accelerated by technological developments, boom and bust grain prices, and inflation. A wider and more advanced variety of seeds, pesticides, herbicides, agricultural implements, and techniques increased both the productivity of farmers and the investment required to produce a crop. The sale of millions of tons of wheat to the Soviet Union in the early 1970s resulted in wheat prices as high as six

Under the watchful eyes of their mothers, youngsters enjoy swimming at the spring opening of the Hillside Park Pool in Bismarck, May 1961. Expanding recreational facilities in North Dakota cities meant North Dakotans could share in the widening and improving standard of living developing in the United States. Courtesy of the SHSND

dollars a bushel. The grain embargo of 1978 and subsequent years caused the price of wheat to plummet to three dollars or less per bushel. Coupled with record high land values, as high as $1,700 an acre in the Red River Valley, high interest rates, expensive equipment, and over-extension of credit, many farmers went belly-up in the late 1970s and 1980s. North Dakota is now losing approximately one thousand farms a year due to economic forces. The crisis prompted many farmers to stage "tractor-cades" to Washington, D.C., and Bismarck. Government was slow to help farmers. New and expanded farm subsidies and state credit and job counseling have helped conditions somewhat.

The fluctuating population that has plagued North Dakota since the 1930s continued up through the 1980s. The state population declined to 619,000 in 1950, rose to 632,000 in 1960, and fell again to 617,000 by 1970. Population zoomed to 652,000 by 1980. Despite the recent growth, lack of economic opportunity still caused thousands to leave the state. By 1983, it was estimated there were approximately 1,000,000 living people born in North Dakota. At that time, only 400,000 lived in North Dakota. The remaining 600,000 had left to seek opportunities and make their homes elsewhere. The remaining 200,000-plus now comprising the state population had moved in from out of state. Incredibly, over half the people born in North Dakota either choose to or must leave the state. Though the

state population was up to approximately 685,000 in 1987 (surpassing the 1930 peak of 680,000), the tragic loss of people, North Dakota's greatest and most valuable resource, seems to be continuing. Increasing numbers of people are outbound today due to the depressed energy economy and a sagging agricultural market.

The twin handicaps of remoteness and isolation that have historically hampered North Dakota's development were largely overcome in the 1960s and 1970s. North Dakota's interstate highway system was completed in 1977, thus linking the state with the rest of the nation through modern automobile transportation. Airline connections increased during the 1960s and 1970s, but dropped off during the 1980s.

Increasing railroad abandonment, especially in the 1970s and 1980s, meant small towns without rail connections declined as larger towns expanded. In 1987, federal census estimates showed that more North Dakotans lived in urban areas (above 2,500 people) than in rural areas for the first time in North Dakota history. Significant exceptions in small town decline were in the "power belt" and "oil patch" towns such as Beulah and Watford City. However, recent trends have caused even these towns to shrink. The consolidation trend continued and accelerated during the 1960s and 1970s. Schools, health and human services, hospitals, and state services had to regionalize.

As in the 1950s and 1960s, massive federal projects in the 1970s and 1980s boosted the North Dakota economy. The specter of diminishing natural gas reserves and the energy crisis of the early 1970s were the impetus for the Great Plains Coal Gasification Project. A relatively economical method to produce synthetic natural gas from lignite was developed and the federal government decided to support an effort to construct the nation's first synfuels plant. North Dakota was selected as the site because of its massive lignite reserves. Construction of the 2.2 billion dollar plant, located outside of Beulah, was initiated in 1980 by the Great Plains Gasification Associates, a consortium of five corporations that planned and financed the plant with loans from the federal government. At the peak of construction activity in 1983, project employment reached nearly 5,800; nine hundred employees are required for normal operation of the plant. Completed in 1984, the plant was producing 92.5 million cubic feet of synthetic natural gas daily by early 1985. At full capacity, the plant can produce 125 million cubic feet each day using fourteen thousand tons of lignite. The U.S. Department of Energy took over the plant in 1986 when the five energy companies that sponsored the project defaulted on a 1.6 billion dollar loan from the federal government. Since then, the Department of Energy has been looking for new owners for the plant; the future of the Great Plains Coal Gasification Project is uncertain.

Manufacturing expanded during the 1960s

North Dakota's "Referral King" Robert P. McCarney is pictured on the right in front of his car dealership in Bismarck, circa 1960. In the 1960s and 1970s, McCarney spearheaded a number of initiated measures and led many referral drives, mostly against state tax increases. McCarney ran for public office a number of times (he was the Republican candidate for governor in 1968), but was never elected. Courtesy of the SHSND

A North Dakota fisherman lands a sauger at the edge of Garrison Dam in the early 1960s. Courtesy of the SHSND

Jackie Kennedy's influence on how American women dressed in the early 1960s is evidenced by the styles sported by these young North Dakota ladies. Courtesy of the SHSND

As always, wheat is king in North Dakota. This 1960 photo shows Virgil Morris in a Baldwin self-propelled combine harvesting Selkirk wheat just north of the state capitol. Courtesy of the SHSND

through the 1980s, but still only accounted for about 5 percent of the gross state product by the late 1980s. Industries locating or expanding in North Dakota included fabricated metal products, lumber and wood products, paper and allied products, leather products, nonelectrical machinery manufacturing, apparel and other textiles, stone, clay and glass products, transportation equipment, electronic equipment, food and kindred products, printing and publishing, and rubber and plastics. Food processing was one of the most logical and successful industrial growth areas with sunflower plants, flour milling, potato processing, sugar refining, barley malting, and pasta processing plants springing up throughout the state, particularly the east. Today thousands of North Dakotans are employed by many manufacturers and other agriculture related industries, such as Amoco Oil Company, Mandan; American Crystal Sugar Company, Drayton; Western Gear, Jamestown; Turtle Mountain Manufacturing Company, Belcourt; and Noodles by Leonardo, Cando. The retail market also increased dramatically during this period. The advent of the shopping mall in all of North Dakota's major cities symbolizes the growth in retail trade.

Exploration of oil and natural gas resources in North Dakota over the last twenty-five years has been profitable as well as controversial. Disagreement over the level of oil and gas development, and the taxation of these industries have occupied the minds and tempers of many North Dakotans. Oil extraction steadily increased and by the early 1980s North Dakota had produced some 710 million barrels of crude oil making the state the ninth largest oil producer in the United States. Currently, North Dakota produces approximately fifty million barrels of oil a year from some three thousand wells. Three oil refineries and seventeen gas plants in the Williston Basin produce 350 million cubic feet of natural gas per day. By the 1980s, estimates of the number of people directly employed in the Williston Basin's oil and gas industry ran as high as eight thousand to twelve thousand. Due to the worldwide oil glut of the 1980s and depressed oil economy, searching and drilling for oil in North Dakota have nearly stopped. Despite this, the oil business looms as one of North Dakota's greatest economic strengths in the future.

Lignite production has also been increasing over the years. North Dakota has a tremendous

President John F. Kennedy received an honorary doctorate from the University of North Dakota on September 25, 1963. In the speech on that occasion, President Kennedy outlined his program for conservation of natural resources in the United States. Less than two months later, President Kennedy was dead, struck down by an assassin's bullet. Courtesy of the SHSND

nite reserve, an estimated 350 billion tons, the eatest coal reserve of any state. Lignite deposits tend over twenty-eight thousand square miles western North Dakota. By the early 1980s, ,694,000 tons of lignite had been produced. All al is strip-mined, and strict state laws require clamation of the land after mining. Approxiately 26 million tons are produced a year with ost of it fed to mine-mouth electrical generating ants that export two-thirds of their power to her states. More than ten electrical generation ants are now operating in North Dakota with a mbined 3,612 megawatt capacity.

The Garrison Diversion Unit project was much odified and has not fared too well in the last enty-five years. After much maneuvering and rangling, Congress authorized a $1.2 billion oject in 1965 to carry Missouri River water to igate 250,000 acres on 1,200 central North akota farms. In addition to irrigation, the project ould provide water relief to cities, develop creational areas, develop fish and wildlife areas, d boost North Dakota's economy. Many opsed the project. Some argued the cost of $1.2 illion to irrigate each farm was too much and at North Dakota farmers did well dry farming

Dr. Anne Carlsen is seen here addressing the annual meeting of the State Historical Society in 1963. She was director of the Crippled Children's School in Jamestown; the school was later named for her. Born without hands or feet, Dr. Anne Carlsen built a national reputation in education for the disabled. Courtesy of the SHSND

most of the time. Conservationists protested the destruction of thousands of wildfowl nesting areas. The Canadian government opposed the project after discovering that Missouri River water would eventually flow into Hudson Bay via the Souris and Red rivers, thus introducing "rough fish" and agricultural pollution to Canadian waters. Construction of a complex system of pumping stations, canals, reservoirs, and pipelines began in 1969. By 1977, the McClusky Canal, seventy-three miles long and connecting Lake Sakakawea with the Lonetree Reservoir, was completed. By the early 1980s, controversy over the Garrison Diversion Unit project stalled additional funding and work. Garrison Diversion continues as one of North Dakota's most serious controversies.

In the political arena, Democrats enjoyed a power and influence never known before. Democrats controlled the governor's office for twenty-eight years (with a single four-year interlude by Republican Gov. Allen Olson) and by 1986 the North Dakota Congressional delegation was solidly democratic. North Dakotans seemed to be comfortable with the new political order and strived to make it work. In spite of democratic successes, North Dakotans still overwhelmingly identify themselves as Republican.

The 1960 elections were great successes for the Democratic-NPL party. William L. Guy defeated the Republican opponent C. P. Dahl, and Quentin Burdick won his first term in the U.S. Senate. William Guy went on to win reelection in 1962 over Mark Andrews, in 1964 over Don Halcrow, and in 1968 over opponent Robert McCarney. Arthur A. Link, a longtime state legislator and member of Congress (elected 1970), was elected governor in 1972 and 1976. Art Link was defeated for reelection by state Attorney General Allen Olson in 1980. Allen Olson suffered defeat by Democrat George Sinner in 1984. The Republicans maintained their legislative hegemony, except during the 1965 session when the Democrats held a House majority for the first time. Other important leaders that started their political careers during the 1960s include Mark Andrews, serving in both the U.S. House of Representatives and the U.S. Senate; Bruce Hagan, a member of the state Public Service Commission from 1961 to the present; and Byron Dorgan, state tax commissioner and later North Dakota's only Representative in the U.S. House.

Longtime Gov. William Guy retired from seeking political office after being narrowly defeated by Milton Young in the 1974 U.S. Senate race. After a recount, it was discovered Guy lost to Young by only 177 votes, the closest Senate race in state history. Milton Young retired in 1981 after serving in the U.S. Senate since 1945.

In the 1970s and 1980s, state leaders were challenged by the major issues of the day, coal development and Garrison Diversion. Leaders struggled to devise policies governing extraction of mineral resources and developed strong

reclamation statutes and high severance fees. State leaders and the congressional delegation labored to follow through on the Garrison Diversion Unit project after the initial appropriation in 1965, but were thwarted by lawsuits and court decisions instigated by environmental groups. Garrison Diversion still remains only a dream to supporters.

North Dakotans also saw the initiative and the referendum become popular tools to control the legislature. In the 1960s and 1970s, Bismarck businessman Robert McCarney spearheaded nine separate ballot drives to reduce state expenditures and taxes. In the 1980s, Dickinson businessman Leon Mallberg assumed McCarney's mantle by leading a number of referral drives in the state.

Since 1960, North Dakotans have favored Republicans over Democrats for president in all but one case. Democrat Lyndon Johnson carried North Dakota against Republican Barry Goldwater in 1964. North Dakotans chose Richard Nixon in 1960, 1968, and 1972; Gerald Ford in 1976; and Ronald Reagan in 1980 and 1984.

The Vietnam War of the 1960s and 1970s was generally supported by North Dakotans. Only a few, small anti-war and anti-draft protests occurred after 1966. Thirty thousand North Dakotans served in the armed forces of the United States during the Vietnam War. Exactly 199 were killed and there are still seventeen MIAs (missing in action). In recognition of North Dakota veterans of all of America's wars since the Civil War, the state of North Dakota has extended a number of benefits to veterans, including bonus payments to veterans of World War II, the Korean War, and the Vietnam War.

North Dakota continued to be in the forefront of America's nuclear defense shield. The air force bases at Minot and Grand Forks continued to expand; Minuteman III ICBMs were installed and B-1 bombers added in the 1980s. An anti-ballistic missile installation was completed at Nekoma in 1974, but closed soon after as the United States and the Soviet Union continued to negotiate for reductions of nuclear weapons.

North Dakotans attempted to reorganize their state in the early 1970s by drafting a new state constitution. The 1889 constitution had been amended approximately one hundred times by 1970 and many felt it was time to rewrite the basic covenant governing the state. In the 1970 primary election, North Dakotans voted to hold a constitutional convention to write a new constitution. The organizational session of the Constitutional Convention convened on April 6, 1971, and elected State Senator Frank A. Wenstrom of Williston as president. Six committees were established to review the constitution and recommend revisions. Following sixteen special public hearings on proposals to the new state constitution, the Constitutional Convention opened in Bismarck on January 3, 1972. The proposed constitution produced by the convention streamlined the government of North Dakota. Major changes in-

uded reducing the number of state elected fficials from fourteen to seven; eliminating the ffice of state auditor and replacing it with an uditor general in the legislative branch; creating state ombudsman; and extending the length of e legislative session. Four other changes or ropositions were adopted and, because controersial, voted on separately: a unicameral legisture, increase in the required number of signares for initiated and referred measures, adult atus for eighteen-to-twenty year olds, and uthorization of certain types of gambling in the ate. After completion of the proposed constitun, the convention adjourned February 17, 1972. blic debate on the proposed constitution was tense. At the special election on April 28, 1972, e proposed constitution was rejected by a vote f 107,643 to 64,073. The votes on the four propoions were mixed. The proposal to establish a nicameral legislature and extend adult status to ghteen-to-twenty year olds failed; the proposin to increase the number of signatures for itiatives and referenda and the authorization of mbling passed. North Dakotans overwhelming rejected the idea of sweeping governmental form. Apparently North Dakotans prefer reform ecemeal as some reforms in the proposed nstitution, such as legalized gambling, have en legislated since the early 1970s.

North Dakotans reformed their state governent in other ways following the failed attempt at nstitutional revision in the 1970s. A state Office Management and Budget was created in 1981 centralize many internal state functions; terms a number of state offices, including the goverr, were extended to four years in the mid-1960s; Department of Labor was created in 1967; and a number of state agencies were reorganized or consolidated. The perceived role of government as an agency of social and economic improvement also widened. North Dakotans authorized creation of special state agencies to deal with development and marketing of agricultural commodities, such as the Wheat Commission, Dairy Products Promotion Commission, Potato Council, Dry Edible Bean Council, Sunflower Council, and the Beef Commission. Due to the rural to urban population shift of the last fifty years, it was necessary during the 1960s and 1970s for North Dakota to reapportion state legislative districts to conform to the principle of "one person, one vote."

Much of the change that has occurred in North Dakota over the last thirty years has largely paralleled the change in the rest of the country. Increasing numbers of women are entering the work force, improved communications, more television and radio stations, improved standards of living, a jump in the divorce rate, improved health care facilities, and improved educational systems are a few factors that affect all Americans. The single greatest change of the last thirty years is that despite our perceptions that we are different from other Americans, more individualistic, tougher, more hard working, and friendlier, we have actually assumed a more standard American character and nature. Though ethnic and religious identities are still great in North Dakota, we have changed, perhaps more than we realize. It can be said we have fully entered the mainstream of American life. This is the achievement of our age.

This man was photographed harvesting sugarbeets in October 1964. The first sugarbeet refinery in North Dakota was established at Drayton in 1965. Courtesy of the SHSND

Its tall, slim tail splitting the horizon like a shark's dorsal fin, this B-52 Stratofortress cruises over a checkered terrain far below. B-52 bombers such as this were assigned to the U.S. Air Force bases at Minot and Grand Forks in the early 1960s. Courtesy of the SHSND

On December 9, 1965, Highway Commissioner Walt Hjelle, Robert Bradley, Robert Strandemo, and Gov. William Guy officially opened Interstate 94 on the Grant Marsh Bridge spanning the Missouri. Completion of the interstate highway system in North Dakota was almost as important as completion in 1879 of the Northern Pacific Railroad across the state in the effect it had in linking North Dakota with the rest of the nation. I-94 and I-29 were complete by 1977. Courtesy of the SHSND

Increasing exploitation of mineral resources in North Dakota was a major trend of the 1950s, 1960s, 1970s, and 1980s. At a trade show, a new product of North Dakota is presented. Eleven major salt beds have been located in North Dakota and commercial production of salt was established in Williston in 1960. Courtesy of the SHSND

The American mania for automobiles can be seen here in downtown Bismarck, looking north on Fourth Street, in the mid-1960s. By 1960, some sixty million passenger cars were registered in the United States. The automobile has changed more than just how Americans travel; it has affected how we shop, our social behavior, the economy, as well as the environment. Courtesy of the SHSND

This 1960s Bucyrus-Erie electric dragline is equipped with a 196-foot boom and a twelve cubic yard bucket. Named the "Beulah Belle," this dragline weights 1,299,000 pounds and is digging in approximately fifty feet of overburden at the Beulah mine of the Knife River Coal Mining Company. Currently, all coal is strip mined in North Dakota. North Dakota's recoverable coal reserve is estimated at sixteen billion tons. Courtesy of the SHSND

The Hazelton High School homecoming queen and attendants ride in style in an open convertible. The rituals and action of high school sporting events were (and still are) a major source of recreation and entertainment for young and old alike in North Dakota. Courtesy of the SHSND

Staged by the Mandan Development Association at Fort Abraham Lincoln, the "Custer Drama" entertained thousands between 1958 and 1968. The play presented a romanticized version of Custer's life at the fort. Courtesy of the SHSND

Youngsters prepare for Halloween in 1960. The quality of life and feeling of security is what many North Dakotans love about their state. Many say North Dakota is a great place to raise children. North Dakota ranks far below the other forty-nine states in violent crimes per one hundred thousand people. Courtesy of the SHSND

Bob Strandemo, general manager of Missouri Valley Motors in Bismarck, presents a Renault "Caravelle" to motorists. Increasing farm income and expanding income in non-agricultural pursuits in the 1960s and 1970s made high-priced products more available to North Dakota consumers. Courtesy of the SHSND

October 31, 1965, marks the inauguration of jet aircraft service by Northwest Airlines in North Dakota. Additional and improved air connections did much to provide another link between North Dakota and the rest of the country. Courtesy of the SHSND

North Dakota's favorite son Lawrence Welk dons a headdress as he is welcomed in a visit to North Dakota. A native of Strasburg, Welk learned the accordion from his father, and in the 1920s began to perform at a radio station in Yankton, South Dakota. Welk had a series of popular dance orchestras in the 1930s and 1940s. Welk achieved national fame with a network musical variety show featuring his "Champagne Music" from 1955 to 1982. Courtesy of the SHSND

Students were leaving classes in Williston Center in this 1963 photo. This branch of the University of North Dakota opened in the late 1950s and served many students in that area. Higher education expanded greatly during this era. Enrollment in the state's colleges and universities in 1960 was just over fourteen thousand. By 1974, enrollment was up to over twenty-seven thousand. State appropriations for higher education mushroomed from less than four million dollars in 1945 to eighty-eight million dollars in 1975. Courtesy of the SHSND

Cradled in the Red River Valley of the North, which was often called the "American Valley of the Nile" because of the fertility of the soil, Grand Forks by 1960 boasted a population of thirty-nine thousand, eight parks, four banks, sixteen thousand telephones, thirty-seven churches, one newspaper, six hotels, sixteen motels, two railroads, two hospitals, and 107 miles of streets with 65.5 percent paved. This aerial view of Grand Forks was taken in 1965. Courtesy of the SHSND

Jamestown's famous Gladstone Hotel burned on March 27, 1968. Built by Anton Klaus, the "father of Jamestown" in 1884, the fire destroyed the first of many significant North Dakota landmarks that were lost in subsequent years, mostly to the wrecking ball. Courtesy of the SHSND

The North Dakota State Fair
at Minot has showcased North
Dakota's agricultural and
industrial achievements as
well as informed and enter-
tained thousands of North
Dakotans for years. Before
1965, a variety of fair associations were authorized by
the Legislative Assembly to
sponsor a state fair. Beginning in the 1890s, state fairs
were held in Grand Forks and
Fargo in alternating years,
and a state fair was authorized in Morton County in
1911 and in Minot in 1923.
The North Dakota State Fair
was created at Minot in 1965.
Courtesy of the SHSND

Dead livestock were found in the aftermath of a blizzard that struck in March 1966. Lasting four days, the storm was forecast well in advance with the result that there was no human loss of life. Blizzards that strike late in winter have been responsible for loss of human life over the years. Over one hundred people died in an 1881 blizzard, thirty-nine in a 1941 blizzard, and several in blizzards in 1975 and 1984. Courtesy of the SHSND

As this button proclaims, the Garrison Diversion project was important to many North Dakotans. The project calls for diversion of Missouri River waters for irrigation of vast tracts of North Dakota, as well as providing water for municipalities. Receiving initial funding and success in the mid and late 1960s and 1970s, momentum for the Garrison Diversion project was lost later in the decade. The future of the Garrison Diversion project is now uncertain. Courtesy of the SHSND

Former Gov. William Guy poses with Gov. Arthur Link in the governor's office in 1973. Art Link succeeded William Guy and served two terms placing the Democratic/NPL Party in control for twenty years. A native of Alexander, Link was a farmer, a longtime state legislator and Speaker of the House during the 1965 legislative session, and served in the U.S. House of Representatives from 1971 to 1973. Art Link lost a reelection race against Republican Allen Olson in 1980. Link is now chairman of the North Dakota Centennial Commission. Courtesy of the SHSND

Gov. William L. Guy welco[mes] King Olav of Norway to N[orth] Dakota in May 1968. Wil[liam] Guy served as governor lo[nger] than any other governor, [...] from 1961 to 1973. A far[mer] and native of Amenia, W[il]liam Guy was the first Democratic/NPL candida[te] successful in reaching the governor's office. As gover[nor] Guy was a tireless advoca[te of] water development and g[ov]ernmental reform. Guy u[n]successfully challenged Mi[lton] Young for a seat in the U.S. Senate in 1974. In the clos[est] U.S. Senate race in North Dakota history, William G[uy] lost to Young by only 177 votes. Later, William Guy served as the director of th[e] Western Governor's Regio[nal] Energy Policy Office and [a] consultant to Basin Electr[ic] Power Cooperative. Courte[sy] of the SHSND

Gov. Arthur Link broke ground for the North Dakota Heritage Center in 1976. State Historical Society Superintendent James Sperry looks on approvingly. Courtesy of the SHSND

On the evening of May 9, 1969, between twenty-five hundred and three thousand young people converged on the small Mercer County town of Zap to engage in what was called a "Zap In." Invited by Zap mayor Norman Fuchs, the high school and college age revelers guzzled beer and broke bottles and windows. The destruction prompted the mayor to ask Governor Guy to send in the National Guard to rout the partiers. The governor ordered the Guard into Zap and peace was restored quickly. The crowd moved to Riverside Park in Bismarck and, joined by many local people, staged a two thousand person beer blast the next night. The National Guard was not invited to the party and the blast blew itself out, leaving truckloads of empty beer cans in its wake. Courtesy of the SHSND

The spectre of diminishing natural gas reserves and the energy crisis of the early 1970s were the impetus for the Great Plains Coal Gasification Project. Completed in 1984, the Great Plains Coal Gasification Plant cost $2.2 billion and converts lignite into synthetic natural gas. Due to financing difficulties, the U.S. Department of Energy now controls the plant and threatens to mothball it if no buyer for the Beulah plant can be found. The future of the Great Plains Coal Gasification plant is uncertain. Courtesy of the SHSND

State Representative Brynhild Haugland has served in the North Dakota House of Representatives continuously since 1939. No female legislator in the United States has served longer than Miss Haugland. A native of Ward County and farm owner near Minot, Miss Haugland is a graduate of Minot State College. She is still serving the people of Ward County in the House to this day. Courtesy of the SHSND

Abortion has long been prohibited by North Dakota state law. The leaflet pictured here was circulated by the North Dakota Abortion Initiative Committee in 1972 urging voters to support an initiated measure to allow abortion in North Dakota. The initiated measure to allow abortions in North Dakota was rejected overwhelmingly by North Dakotans, 204,852 to 62,604. The following year, a U.S. Supreme Court decision rendered North Dakota's anti-abortion laws null and void. Courtesy of the SHSND

Vote "YES" for the North Dakota Abortion Initiative Nov. 7

**PARTIAL LIST OF ORGANIZATIONS
WHICH HAVE TAKEN OFFICIAL POSITIONS IN FAVOR OF
MAKING ABORTION AN INDIVIDUAL DECISION**

American Baptist Convention
American Lutheran Church (Church Council)
Church Women United, Board of Managers
Episcopal Churchwomen of the U.S.A.
Lutheran Church of America
United Church of Christ
United Methodist Church, U.S.A
United Presbyterian Church of U.S.A.
American Bar Association
National Conference of Commissioners on Uniform State Laws
American College of Obstetrics and Gynecology
American Medical Association
American Protestant Hospital Association
American Public Health Association
American Psychiatric Association
National Council of Obstetrics and Gynecology
National Medical Association
American Association of University Women
Commission on Population Growth and the American Future
Izaak Walton League (National)
National Committee on Children and Youth
National Conference on Family Relations
National Council of Women of the United States
National Council on Crime and Delinquency
Planned Parenthood
President's Task Force on the Mentally Handicapped
Sierra Club
Young Women's Christian Association (YWCA)

Gallup Poll results: 64% of Americans, including 56% of Catholics, agreed that "the decision to have an abortion should be made solely by a woman and her physician."

83% of obstetricians polled agreed with the official stand of the American College of Obstetricians and Gynecologists recommending that abortion be performed upon a patient's request.

The North Dakota Abortion Initiative Committee is currently seeking the assistance of all North Dakota residents. We need people to help work in their communities, and money to defray printing costs and other campaign expenses. Won't you help take our message to others?

I will make a contribution. Enclosed is ___$2. ___$5. ___$10. ___25. ___$
I will help your education effort by leafleting in my community.
Other ___

NAME _____ ADDRESS _____

N.D. Abortion Initiative Committee
Box 1192
Bismarck, N.D. 58501

Pol Ad Pd & Sp by NDAIC R Kashmark M.D. inform dir

...rth Dakota retailers show...r wares at a convention in...go in 1972. Retail trade in...rth Dakota cities has been...the increase over the last...enty-five years, as evi-...nced by the rise of shopping...lls in North Dakota cities...d the convenience of the...tomobile to transport...oppers to the stores. Courtesy...the SHSND

This grain elevator was photographed in Butte, McLean County, in 1976. Due to the rural to urban population shift, many small North Dakota towns are slowly drying up. Courtesy of the SHSND

This livestock auction took place in 1973. Focused in the western part of the state, livestock and livestock products were valued at approximately $700 million in 1985. Courtesy of the SHSND

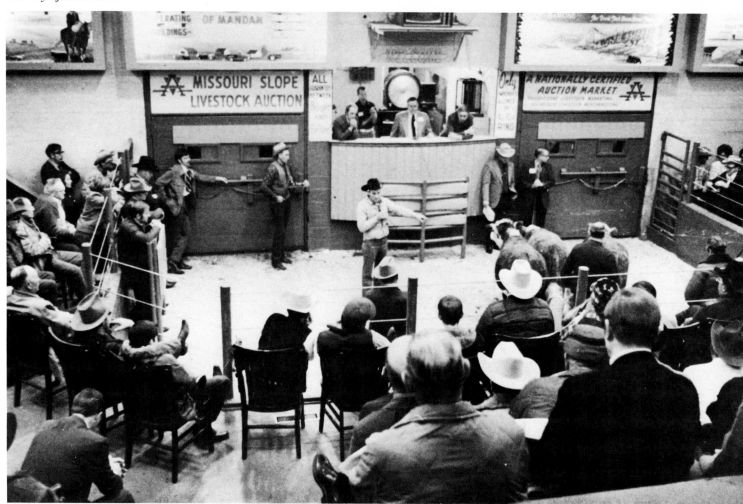

Approximately three hundred
missile silos containing
Minuteman III ICBMs are
clustered around Minot and
Grand Forks. Signs on the gate
of each silo site warn would-be
intruders to take their curiosity
elsewhere. The presence of
these nuclear weapons puts
North Dakota in the forefront
of America's defensive and
offensive capabilities. Photo by
David Gray

Bishop John F. Kinney of the
Roman Catholic Diocese of
Bismarck blesses the fields and
soil in a "Town and Country"
celebration in 1984. North
Dakotans exhibit one of the
highest levels of church
attendance in the United
States. Seventy-one percent of
North Dakotans belong to a
church: 46.7 percent are
Protestant and 24.2 percent
are Roman Catholic. Lutherans (all bodies) are the largest
denomination comprising 33
percent of all church membership. Courtesy John Owens,
Roman Catholic Diocese of
Bismarck archives

The number of family farms has been decreasing at a steady rate over the last thirty years, from approximately fifty-five thousand in 1960 to about thirty-three thousand today. What this trend means for the future of agriculture in North Dakota is uncertain. Courtesy of Sheldon Green

North Dakota has been a principal cow-calf producing state for years. North Dakota presently ranks seventeenth in the nation for all cattle, twenty-seventh for milk cows, and twelfth for beef cows. Courtesy of the N.D. Tourism Promotion Division

Despite the current slump in the oil industry, oil remains and will continue to be important to the North Dakota economy. Mineral industries added $1.3 billion to the North Dakota economy in 1986. Extraction of oil and natural gas generated $900 million of that amount. Courtesy of Robert Knutsen Photography

Roughnecks manhandle an oil drilling rig. Courtesy of Sheldon Green

Ranching is a growing industry in North Dakota, especially in the west. The value of North Dakota farm products was $2.8 billion in 1985; 75 percent was derived from crops and 25 percent from livestock and livestock products. Courtesy of the SHSND

French horns blare in unison as North Dakota musicians celebrate the wonder of their craft. Local and community orchestras and bands have been a long tradition in North Dakota. Expanding opportunities in music, theatre, and dance benefit and enrich the lives of all North Dakotans. Courtesy of the SHSND

A Melroe "Bobcat" loader is assembled in the Bismarck Melroe Division, Clark Equipment Company plant. Manufacturing accounts for an increasing amount of our gross state product. Representing only about 5 percent of our economy by the 1980s, manufacturing contributes approximately $483 million to the state's economy. In 1986, an out-of-state firm consulting with the state declared North Dakota had the best manufacturing climate in the nation. Courtesy of Sheldon Green

A physician examines X-rays in a North Dakota medical center. Medical facilities have expanded greatly in North Dakota over the last twenty-five years. Bismarck, Fargo, and Grand Forks boast major medical centers. North Dakota has fifty-nine hospitals with approximately six thousand beds and many excellent health care practitioners. As a result, North Dakotans enjoy longer and healthier lives. The average life expectancy is now sixty-nine years for men and seventy-seven years for women, compared to sixty-seven years and seventy-four years nationally. Courtesy of the SHSND

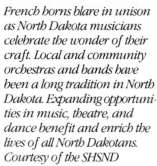
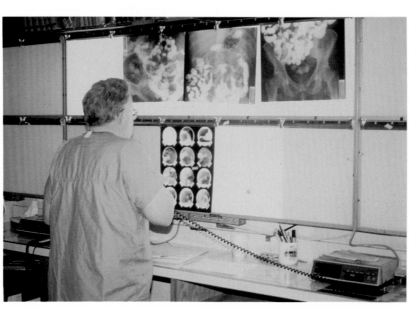

Graduates of North Dakota secondary schools earn top scores on national collegiate entrance examinations due to the excellence of the schools. North Dakotans have worked long and hard to produce some of the best schools in the country. Presently, the educational system in North Dakota consists of some 310 public school districts, 104 nonpublic schools, and 9 Bureau of Indian Affairs schools with a total enrollment of nearly 130,000 students, taught and administered by ten thousand educational professionals. Courtesy of the SHSND

The Coal Creek Power Plant is located at Underwood. Approximately twenty-six million tons of lignite are mined each year with most of it fed to mine-mouth electrical generating plants, such as the Underwood plant. The plants export two-thirds of their power to other states. More than ten electrical generation plants are now operating in North Dakota with a combined 3,612 megawatt capacity. Courtesy of the N.D. Tourism Promotion Division

Marv Brossert of WDAY-TV, Fargo, prepares for a news broadcast. North Dakotans strive to keep informed of current events. By the late 1980s, North Dakota had sixteen television stations, fifty-three radio stations, and ninety weekly and ten daily newspapers. Courtesy of the SHSND

Competitive dancing is a major attraction of the pow-wows held in North Dakota each year. The colorful dancers are judged on their skill and the authenticity of their raiment. Native Americans now account for about 2 percent of the population of North Dakota. Courtesy of the N.D. Tourism Promotion Division

The striking interior of the Kirkwood Mall in Bismarck symbolizes the preeminence of the shopping mall in retailing, not just in North Dakota, but in the entire country as well. Retail sales in North Dakota totaled $4.3 billion in 1985, with groceries accounting for $579 million and automobile dealers garnering $1.3 billion. Courtesy of the SHSND

A Steiger Tractor is shown being assembled at the Fargo plant. Invented by the Steiger brothers in 1957, Steiger Tractor, Inc. moved to Fargo from Minnesota in 1969.

Steiger Tractor filed for bankruptcy in 1986 and was purchased by Tenneco. Steiger Tractor, Inc., still builds Steiger tractors, but is operated by Case IH. The Fargo plant cur-

rently employs 280 workers, down from an employment high of around 1,000 in 1975. Courtesy of the N.D. Tourism Promotion Division

Lake Sakakawea, the reservoir behind Garrison Dam on the Missouri River, is the largest lake in North Dakota and the largest man-made lake wholly within one state. Boating and water sports abound at Lake Sakakawea, where the entire shoreline is open to the public. Pleasure boats, fishing boats, sailboats, and canoes are commonly seen on "the Big Lake." Courtesy of the N.D. Tourism Promotion Division

Irrigation assists many North Dakota farmers in achieving maximum yields. Approximately 212,700 acres are presently under irrigation; over 6 million acres of land are potentially irrigable. Many North Dakotans dream of massive irrigation projects, such as the Garrison Diversion Project, that will eliminate the effects of dry years, help take some of the risk out of farming, and make farm income more stable. Massive irrigation today is still just a dream to many North Dakotans. Courtesy of the SHSND

Sunflowers are a major cash crop in North Dakota. Sunflower seeds have uses other than as food and oil. At the National Sun Industries sunflower processing plant at Enderlin, a power plant adjacent to the sunflower plant uses sunflower hulls as fuel for electrical power generation. The power plant can produce up to nine thousand kilowatts at full capacity. The surplus power flows to the Otter Tail Power Company for distribution to other customers. Courtesy of the HSND

Wheat is King in North Dakota, ranking first in the United States in production of durum wheat, first in spring wheat, and only second to Kansas in all wheat production. North Dakota also ranks first in production in oats, potatoes, and sugar beets; ninth in oil and American cheese; and twelfth in coal. Courtesy of the N.D. Tourism Promotion Division

The North Dakota State University (NDSU) Bison football team won the NCAA Division 2 championships in 1965, 1968, 1969, 1983, 1985, and 1986. Formerly the North Dakota Agricultural College until 1960, NDSU now has ten thousand students, six hundred faculty, and eighty buildings covering nearly thirty square blocks. Courtesy of the SHSND

North Dakota wetlands are crucial to the survival of millions of migratory wildfowl. The Central Waterfowl Flyway lies over much of North Dakota. Hundreds of thousands of Canada geese, mallards, pintail, gadwell, scaup ducks, gulls, herons, pelicans, and other birds fly through, feed, and roost in North Dakota wetlands. Courtesy of Craig Bihrle, N.D. Game and Fish Department

The American elm, "Ulmus americana," is a favorite shade tree of city streets, parks, and college campuses. It grows up to 120 feet tall and has a characteristic wineglass shape. The American elm was named the official state tree by the 1947 Legislative Assembly. Courtesy of Edward Bry, N.D. Game and Fish Department

NORTH DAKOTA SYMBOLS

There are many symbols, places, and things we associate with North Dakota. State symbols remind us of who we are, our history, the way we live, and the beauty of our state. Symbols are often a focal point for the pride we feel in North Dakota.

North Dakota has many official state symbols. Others, though not officially established as state symbols by the Legislative Assembly, are meaningful to North Dakotans and are pictured here.

The western meadowlark, "Sturnella neglecta," is a common bird of North Dakota prairies, and is often seen perching on road signs. It has a loud, ringing, flute-like song. This sociable bird belongs to the same family as the bobolink and the blackbirds. The western meadowlark was named the official state bird in 1947. Courtesy of Edward Bry, N.D. Game and Fish Department

GREAT SEAL

LIBERTY AND UNION NOW AND FOREVER ONE AND INSEPARABLE

OCTOBER 1st

1889

STATE OF NORTH DAKOTA.

The Great Seal of North Dakota was prescribed by Section 207 of the North Dakota Constitution in 1889. It is based on the Great Seal of the Territory of Dakota, adopted between 1862 and 1863. Courtesy of the SHSND

The state crest or the Governor's Coat of Arms combines yellow-gold and green, indicative of the great agricultural state of North Dakota. The Indian arrowhead forms the shield and symbolizes the "Sioux State." The three stars denote the branches of state government: legislative, executive, and judicial. The stars also allude to the history of the Territory under three foreign flags. The fleur-de-lis refers to La Verendrye, the French explorer who was the first known white man to visit the territory of the state. The state crest was created by the Legislative Assembly in 1957. Courtesy of the SHSND

Except for the name North Dakota replacing the original regimental name, the North Dakota state flag is the same as that used by the First North Dakota Infantry. The infantry flag was carried into battle during the Spanish-American War and the Philippine Insurrection. The state flag was officially adopted in 1911 by the Legislative Assembly. The state attempted to devise a new state flag between 1951 and 1953, but the new design was rejected by the Legislative Assembly. The present state flag was officially confirmed and described by the Legislative Assembly in 1959. Courtesy of the SHSND

The wild prairie rose, "Rosa blanda or arkansana," was adopted as the state flower by the Legislative Assembly in 1907. Courtesy of the N.D. Tourism Promotion Division

The northern pike, "Esox lucius," is an outstanding, tasty game fish. Although most are under fifteen pounds when caught, the record weighted thirty-seven pounds, eight ounces. It was caught at Lake Sakakawea in 1968. The fish pictured here was caught in 1985 and weighed thirty-one pounds, four ounces. The northern pike was established as the state fish by the Legislative Assembly in 1969. Courtesy of Edward Bry, N.D. Game and Fish Department

Western wheatgrass, "Agropyron smithii," is a tough, native prairie grass that once covered most of the state. It was named the official state grass by the Legislative Assembly in 1977. Courtesy of the SHSND

Teredo bored petrified wood is a reminder of a time when warm-water bays and coastal swamps were part of the North Dakota landscape. Some sixty to eighty million years ago, pieces of wood fell into the warm waters and were invaded by teredos, worm-shaped mollusks that are related to clams, mussels, and oysters. As the wood remained in the mineral-rich water, and was covered with earth, some pieces were petrified. The woody material was replaced by silica or quartz. Teredo bored petrified wood was officially named the state fossil by the Legislative Assembly in 1967. Courtesy of the SHSND

Milk was established as the official state
beverage by the Legislative Assembly in 1983.
Courtesy of the SHSND

James W. Foley, known as the "poet of North
Dakota," wrote the words of the "North
Dakota Hymn" in 1926. Dr. C.S. Putnam,
then head of the music department at North
Dakota State Agricultural College, wrote an
original score for the words. Together, both the
original words and music are now the official state song. The first stanza:

North Dakota, North Dakota,
With thy prairies wide and free,
All thy sons and daughters love thee,
Fairest state from sea to sea;

North Dakota, North Dakota,
Here we pledge ourselves to thee.
North Dakota, North Dakota,
Here we pledge ourselves to thee.

"The Flickertail" was commissioned by the
Legislative Assembly in 1975. Composed by
James D. Ployhar, it is played at appropriate
state functions.

The State Capitol grounds were first established in 1883 when the capital of Dakota Territory was transferred to Bismarck. Today the State Capitol Complex hosts the State Capitol, State Highway Building, Liberty Memorial Building, the Heritage Center, and statuary on the grounds. Courtesy of Mike Lalonde

The North Dakota State Capitol was completed by 1934. The original 1883 capitol was destroyed by fire in 1930. The original west wing houses the legislature, the executive branch occupies the tower, and the judicial branch and other agencies occupy the east wing, dedicated in 1981. Courtesy of the N.D. Tourism Promotion Division

Shown here is the grand opening of the North Dakota Heritage Center on June 28, 1981. The North Dakota Heritage Center is home to the State Archives and Historical Research Library, and facilities for archeology, historic preservation, museum, and historic sites. Courtesy of the N.D. Tourism Promotion Division

Constructed in 1924, the Liberty Memorial Building was dedicated to those who served in World War I. The State Historical Society occupied the Liberty Memorial Building until 1981, when it was renovated for the State Library and the Economic Development Commission. Courtesy of the N.D. Tourism Promotion Division

Commemorating over 170 years of peace between the United States and Canada, the International Peace Garden symbolizes that two nations can live in peace and harmony along the longest unfortified boundary in the world. The International Peace Garden lies on the border of North Dakota and Manitoba in the Turtle Mountains area. Dedicated in 1932, the International Peace Garden comprises over twenty-three hundred acres of gardens. North Dakota gets its nickname, the "Peace Garden State" from the International Peace Garden. Courtesy of the N.D. Tourism Promotion Division

The Richardson ground squirrel is often called the flickertail, and from it North Dakota gets its nickname, "The Flickertail State." Courtesy of Edward Bry, N.D. Game and Fish Department

Money for the statue of Sakakawea, Lewis and Clark's Shoshoni guide, was raised by children and clubwomen of North Dakota. Leonard Crunelle sculpted the statue and it was erected on the capitol grounds and presented to the state in 1910. Courtesy of the SHSND

The pioneer family statue on the capitol
grounds was presented to North Dakota as a
gift from Harry F. McLean in 1947. Sculpted
by Avard Fairbanks, the statue is a tribute to
those who settled in North Dakota. Courtesy
of the SHSND

The geographical center of North Dakota lies near Rugby in Pierce County. This obelisk marks the approximate spot. Courtesy of the N.D. Tourism Promotion Division

1450 Mandan Indians began fortifying their villages.

1670 Hudson's Bay Company received its royal charter; by 1672 the company was trading at York Factory on the Bay (Canada).

1682 LaSalle, French explorer, claimed part of what is now North Dakota drained by the Missouri River for France.

1738 French explorer Pierre de La Verendrye made the first known Euro-American exploration into what is now North Dakota, visiting Mandan villages on the Missouri River.

1742 Verendrye's sons returned to the Missouri River searching for a western sea.

1762 France transferred land claimed by LaSalle to Spain.

1763 England obtained title to the state drained by the Mouse and Red Rivers.

1768 Jonathon Carver explored through the Red River Valley for the Provincial Government.

1776 United States declared its independence from Great Britain.

1790 Jacques d'Eglise, a Saint Louis trader, reached Mandan territory.

1794 Rene Jesseaume established Jesseaume's Post for the North West Company. Saint Louis merchants formed the Missouri Company and sent three expeditions to North Dakota, 1794-1795.

1796 The Missouri Company took possession of Jesseaume's Post.

1797 David Thompson, English geographer, explored and mapped the Mouse and Missouri River basins; Charles Chaboillez of the North West Company established the first fur trading post at Park River.

1798 Roy's Post was built at the mouth of the Forest River (also called the Salt River) for the North West Company.

1800 Spain ceded Louisiana Territory back to France. Alexander Henry, Jr., opened a fur trading post at Park River.

1801 Alexander Henry, Jr., moved his trading post to Pembina. Henry sent a crew to Grandes Fourches (Grand Forks) to establish a post. The X Y Company built a post at Pembina.

1802 On March 12, the first non-Indian child in the state, a girl, was born to Pierre Bonza and wife. They were blacks, employed at Henry's post at Pembina. Charles le Raye explored western North Dakota that year while a captive of the Sioux. John Cameron built the Turtle River Post for the North West Company.

1803 Louisiana Purchase made southwestern North Dakota part of the United States.

1804-6 Lewis and Clark, accompanied by Sakakawea, crossed North Dakota on their journey to the Pacific. Fort Mandan was built in 1804 for their winter stay at the Mandan villages.

1809 Manuel Lisa set out from Saint Louis in May in search of suitable sites for trading posts along the Missouri River. A member of the Missouri Fur Company, Lisa built Fort Manuel Lisa on the west side of the Missouri above the mouth of the Knife River. On December 29, the first white child in the state was born in Pembina.

1811 John Bradbury and Thomas Nuttal, English botanists, joined the Astoria Overland expedition up the Missouri and Yellowstone rivers to Oregon.

1812 Selkirk colonists came to Pembina to make the first attempt at white settlement in the state. John McLeod built a post at Turtle River for the Hudson's Bay Company. North Dakota became part of Missouri Territory.

1813 Manuel Lisa abandoned his fort near the Knife River villages at the outbreak of the War of 1812.

1818 Father Dumoulin and Father Provencher opened the first church in the state, a Roman Catholic mission at Pembina. The first school, taught by William Edge, was begun in connection with this mission. The United States acquired eastern North Dakota by treaty with England.

1820 Grasshoppers destroyed the Red River Valley crops.

1821 The North West Company and the Hudson's Bay Company merge.

1822 Gen. W. H. Ashley and other explorers established fur trading posts in the Missouri River Valley. James Kipp built Fort Tilton for the Columbia Fur Company.

1823 James Kipp established Fort Mandan across the river from Fort Tilton after being driven out by the Arikara. Gen. William Ashley and Andrew Henry of the Rocky Mountain Fur Company built Ashley and Henry's Post. Gen. Stephen H. Long's survey expedition designated the official boundary between the United States and Canada at a point north of Pembina. Selkirk colonists left Pembina and moved to Canadian soil. Gen. Henry Leavenworth came up the Missouri to make treaties with the Arikara and other Indians.

1824 Atkinson-O'Fallon Expedition to the Knife River.

1825 Gen. Henry Atkinson visited this area on a military expedition. James Kipp established the White Earth River Post (also called Kipp's Post, or Fort Kipp) for the Columbia Fur Company. First treaty between the U.S. and the Mandan and Hidatsa.

1828 Kenneth McKenzie built Fort Floyd for the American Fur Company; later renamed Fort Union in 1829.

1831 Fort Clark was built on the Missouri River by James Kipp of the American Fur Company.

1832 *Yellowstone,* first steamboat to navigate the Missouri River in North Dakota, made a voyage to Fort Union. Col. Henry Leavenworth signed a treaty with the Arikara.

1833 Maximilian, Prince of Wied, conducted a scientific expedition up the Missouri. Artist George Catlin explored the region, 1832-1834.

1836 North Dakota became part of Wisconsin Territory.

1837 Smallpox epidemic nearly wiped out the Mandan Indian tribe.

1838 North Dakota became part of Iowa Territory.

1839 John C. Fremont and Jean N. Nicollet led the first exploration through central North Dakota. Father Pierre Jean De Smet began missionary work among North Dakota Indians and persuaded the Sioux to take part in peace councils.

1842 First Red River ox-cart caravan traversed trails between Saint Joseph (Walhalla) and Saint Paul, inaugurating a major commerce that continued for over twenty-five years. Joseph Rolette opened an American Fur Company post at Pembina.

1843 Rival post was built at Pembina by Norman Kittson. John James Audubon, naturalist, studied North Dakota animal life. Antoine Gingras built a trading post in the Pembina area.

1844 Norman Kittson opened a trading post at Pembina.

1845 Bartholomew Berthold founded the American Fur Company post named for himself on the Missouri River.

1848 Father George Belcourt opened mission fields at Pembina, Walhalla, and the Turtle Mountains. The Reverend Alonzo Barnard and James Tanner conducted the first Protestant church services in the state at Pembina. The first printing press was brought to North Dakota by Barnard.

1849 The Hudson's Bay Company's monopoly of the area ended.

1851 First North Dakota post office was established at Pembina with Norman Kittson as postmaster. He erected the Kittson House, a trading post and warehouse. Charles Cavilier brought settlers from Minnesota to Pembina to form the first permanent agricultural colony in the state. First flour mill in the state was constructed by Father Belcourt at Walhalla.

1853 Stevens' survey expedition, sponsored by the federal government, passed through North Dakota seeking a railroad route. Official U.S. government mail service began in Pembina.

1857 Fort Abercrombie, first military post in North Dakota, was established on the Red River. The fort was abandoned in 1859 and reoccupied in 1860.

1859 On January 5, the *Anson Northrop,* first Red River steamboat, started a trip from Fort Abercrombie to Winnipeg.

1860 Regular steamboat transportation began on the upper Missouri.

1861 Dakota Territory was officially organized. President Lincoln appointed William Jayne first governor of Dakota Territory. American Civil War begins.

1862 First territorial legislature met in Yankton. Sioux Uprising occurs. Refugees fled to Fort Abercrombie; the Fort is besieged. Little Crow and his followers sought refuge with the Sioux at Devils Lake. Capt. James L. Fisk and Thomas A. Holmes guided parties across North Dakota to the Montana gold fields.

1863 January 1, Dakota Territory opened for homesteading. Gen. Henry H. Sibley and Gen. Alfred H. Sully were sent to punish the Sioux who took part in the Sioux Uprising. Sibley Expedition (battles of Big Mound, Dead Buffalo Lake, Stony Lake). Sully Expedition (Battle of Whitestone Hill).

1864 The first North Dakota newspaper, the *Frontier Scout,* was issued at Fort Union. General Sully established Fort Rice. Emigrant party under Captain Fisk came under seige by the Sioux at Fort Dilts. Sully Expedition against the Sioux continues with the Battle of Killdeer Mountains.

1865 Civil War ends. Sully Expedition against the Sioux continues.

1866 Fort Buford established on the Missouri opposite the mouth of the Yellowstone River.

1867 Fort Ransom, second in a chain of forts for protection of emigrant trains, was established on the Sheyenne River by

Gen. Alfred H. Terry. Forts Stevenson and Totten, and Fort Totten Indian Reservation established. Treaty with the Sisseton and Wahpeton Sioux gave the United States rights to build roads and railroads across Indian lands. Pembina County was created.

68   Influenced by Father De Smet, the Sioux joined the peace council at Fort Rice. The Laramie Treaty defined Sioux Indian Reservation boundaries, including the Standing Rock Reservation. Joseph Rolette made the first North Dakota homestead entry, filing on land in the northwestern part of the Red River Valley.

70   Fort Berthold Indian Reservation boundaries were defined. The treaty between the Chippewa, Sioux, and whites at Fort Abercrombie brought permanent peace to the eastern part of the state. Fort Pembina was built. Capt. Alexander Griggs plotted Grand Forks.

71   Northern Pacific Railway reached Fargo. First North Dakota telegraph line was put into operation between Fort Abercrombie and Winnipeg. The Whistler expedition began a survey of railway lines westward through North Dakota. Squatters began occupying land along the Red River where the Northern Pacific Railroad planned to cross the river.

72   Northern Pacific Railroad built from the Red River to Jamestown. Fort Seward replaced Fort Ransom. Fort McKeen was built on the Missouri River and later included in Fort Abraham Lincoln. Camp Hancock established.

73   Fort Abraham Lincoln was built. Bismarck became the "end of the line" of the Northern Pacific Railway. On July 11, Col. C. A. Lounsberry published the first issue of the *Bismarck Tribune,* the state's oldest newspaper still in existence. The counties of Bottineau, Burleigh, Cass, Cavalier, Foster, Grand Forks, Kidder, Logan, LaMoure, McHenry, Mountrail, Ramsey, Ransom, Renville, Richland, Rolette, Sheridan, Stutsman, and Wells were established.

74   The United States Weather Bureau was established as part of Camp Hancock in Bismarck. The *Fargo Express,* the first newspaper in the Red River Valley, was printed at Fargo. The Black Hills Expedition led by George A. Custer and the Seventh Cavalry; Custer verified report of gold in the Black Hills. First commercial lignite mine opened at Fort Abraham Lincoln.

75   Era of Bonanza farming began. The War Department permitted whites to settle on reservations in violation of the Laramie Treaty, precipitating uprisings among the Sioux. Fort Yates was built. War Department ordered all Indians to report to Indian agencies.

1876   On May 17, Gen. George Armstrong Custer left Fort Abraham Lincoln on the Little Big Horn campaign. On June 25, Custer and his immediate command were annihilated by Indians consisting largely of the Sioux at the Battle of the Little Big Horn.

1877   Fort Seward was abandoned. First telephone in northern Dakota connected locations on the Grandin bonanza farm near Grandin.

1878   Fort Yates was established to succeed Fort Rice. Ranching was introduced into the western part of North Dakota. Fort Abercrombie was abandoned.

1879   The Great Dakota Boom began.

1880   James J. Hill began building the Great Northern Railway through the state. Lignite mining was begun in western North Dakota. Military reserves in the eastern and central parts of the state were opened to homesteaders.

1881   Sitting Bull surrendered at Fort Buford. Northern Pacific reached the Montana border. Population of northern Dakota was 36,909.

1882   The Great Northern Railway was completed through the Red River Valley to Canada. The Turtle Mountain Reservation was established for the Chippewa Indians.

1883   The Dakota territorial capital was moved from Yankton to Bismarck. Jamestown College was established, and the University of North Dakota opened at Grand Forks. The Marquis de Mores opened his packing plant at Medora. Theodore Roosevelt came to North Dakota for his health and began to ranch near Medora. The first labor union in North Dakota was formed at Bismarck. Fort Stevenson was abandoned.

1885   The Hospital for the Insane opened in Jamestown. Territorial Penitentiary opened at Bismarck. The Great "Dakota Boom" in settlement increased population during this era.

1886   The Bank of Hamilton was founded; it later became the first state bank.

1887   A treaty with the Sioux allowed whites to settle on Standing Rock Indian Reservation. The Great Northern Railway reached the Montana border.

1889   February 22, Congress passed the Enabling Act, and on July 4 the State Constitutional Convention opened at Bismarck. The State Constitution was adopted on October 1, and on November 2 President Harrison admitted North Dakota to statehood. The Constitution made North Dakota a "dry" state. John Miller took office as the first governor. The first Legislative Assembly met at Bismarck on November 19. Roman Catholic Diocese of Jamestown, later Fargo, was established.

1890   The State Normal School opened at Valley City, the State Agricultural College at Fargo, the State Normal School at Mayville, and the School for the Deaf at Devils Lake. Andrew Burke was elected governor. Fort Totten was abandoned. Panic among white settlers stemming from Ghost Dance activities among Sioux rushed through western North Dakota. Sioux leader Sitting Bull was killed on the Standing Rock Indian Reservation.

1891   A severe drought prevailed throughout the state. Fort Abraham Lincoln was abandoned.

1892   Eli Shortridge, Populist, was elected governor on a fusion ticket in reaction to interference by railway companies in state politics. Laura J. Eisenhuth, first woman to hold state office, was elected Superintendent of Public Instruction.

1893   Industrial School at Ellendale (later State Normal and Industrial School) was established.

1894   Roger Allin, Republican, was elected governor.

1895   Fort Pembina and Fort Buford were abandoned. State Historical Commission was created.

1896   Frank Briggs, Republican, was elected governor.

1897   First free public library in the state opened at Grafton. The Industrial and Normal School at Ellendale opened.

1898   Governor Briggs died and Lt. Gov. Joseph M. Devine completed the term. Fred B. Fancher, Republican, was elected governor. Spanish-American War begins. North Dakota National Guard was federalized. Much of Bismarck was destroyed by fire.

1900   Frank White, Republican, was elected governor.

1902   Governor White was reelected. Arthur Basset and Arthur Le Sueur established the North Dakota Socialist Party.

1903   New Fort Lincoln was built and garrisoned. Fort Yates was abandoned.

1904   The State School of Science opened at Wahpeton, and the School for the

Feeble-minded (later named Grafton State School) opened at Grafton. E. Y. Sarles, Republican, was elected govern[or]

1905   State Historical Society of North Dakota given legal status.

1906   John Burke, Democrat, was elected governor.

1907   State School of Forestry opened at Bottineau.

1909   First state child labor law was enacted. The State Library Commission was created.

1910   John Burke, Democrat, was first govern[or] to be reelected to a third term. The U.S.S North Dakota was commissioned. State population reached 577,146.

1911   State Hail Insurance fund was created (abolished in 1967).

1912   L.B. Hanna, Republican, was elected governor.

1913   The State Normal School opened at Minot. State Highway Commission created.

1914   World War I began in Europe.

1915   The Nonpartisan League (NPL) was organized in February.

1916   Lynn J. Frazier was elected first Nonpartisan League Governor. NPL gains co[n]trol of most state offices and the state House of Representatives. Oil exploration begins in North Dakota.

1917   United States enters World War I. North Dakota National Guard was federalized.

1918   The State Normal School opened at Dic[k]inson. Seven initiated amendments based on the Nonpartisan League platform were approved by the voters.

1919   The Bank of North Dakota was organized. The Industrial Commission was created. State Workers' Compensation Bureau was formed. The State Mill and Elevator Association was created.

1920   The Recall Measure was passed. On April 29, the contract was let for the State Mill and Elevator at Grand Forks. Lynn J. Frazier, NPL, was reelected to a third ter[m] as governor. State population reached 646,872.

1921   Governor Frazier was recalled. He was succeeded by R. A. Nestos, I.V.A. Republican.

1922   Governor Frazier was elected to the United States Senate. WDAY, first North Dakota radio station, was opened at Fargo. The first bus line in the state was established.

1924   Arthur G. Sorlie, NPL, was elected governor.

25   Gerald P. Nye was appointed to fill the United States Senate vacancy caused by the death of Sen. E. F. Ladd.

27   Governor Sorlie died. He was succeeded by Lt. Gov. Walter Maddock. North Dakota Farmers' Union chartered.

28   George F. Shafer, I.V.A. Republican, was elected governor. Air mail service between the Twin Cities and Winnipeg, through North Dakota, was inaugurated.

29   Prolonged drought throughout North-west began.

30   State Capitol destroyed by fire, December 28. State population reached 680,845.

32   Cornerstone of new $2 million capitol dedicated on October 8 by Vice-President Charles M. Curtis. William Langer, NPL, was elected governor. The prohibition clause of the State Constitution was repealed.

33   Governor Langer proclaimed moratoriums on mortgage foreclosure sales and shipment of farm commodities from North Dakota, and a state bank holiday.

34   On July 18, the North Dakota Supreme Court held Governor Langer disqualified for office; Lt. Gov. Ole H. Olson became governor.

35   On January 7, Thomas H. Moodie, Democrat, was inaugurated governor. On February 2, the North Dakota Supreme Court declared Moodie ineligible. Walter Welford, NPL, lieutenant governor, became governor. The State Welfare and State Planning boards were created. The state government moved into the new State Capitol. The "Nye Committee" began hearings on munitions makers.

36   William Langer defeated Welford for governorship. Sale of liquor was legalized in North Dakota by referendum vote. President Franklin D. Roosevelt visited the state and toured drought-stricken areas in August. William Lemke of North Dakota ran for president on the Union party ticket.

937   Water Conservation Commission was established.

938   John Moses, Democrat, was elected governor. First hard-surfaced highway across North Dakota (U.S. 10) completed.

939   War began in Europe.

940   The State Staff of the North Dakota National Guard was ordered into federal service. John Moses was reelected governor. State population dips to 641,935.

941   Several divisions of the North Dakota National Guard were ordered into federal service. Thirty-nine people in North Dakota killed in a blizzard in the Red River Valley. The United States entered World War II.

1942   Gov. John Moses was reelected to a third term. The North Dakota Farm Bureau was created.

1943   North Dakota led in per-capita U.S. War Bond sales. Republican Organizing Committee (ROC) organized. The U.S.S. *Grand Forks* was commissioned.

1944   Fred G. Aandahl, ROC, was elected governor. The state placed first in the nation in the production of spring wheat, durum, barley and acres of certified seed potatoes. The Pick-Sloan Plan for control of the Missouri River Basin was approved by Congress.

1945   World War II ends. Sen. John Moses dies in office; Gov. Fred Aandahl appoints Milton Young to fill the seat.

1946   Construction of Garrison Dam began.

1947   President Harry S Truman signed the bill providing for the Theodore Roosevelt National Memorial Park in North Dakota. A state law facilitating school consolidation was enacted.

1948   Gov. Fred G. Aandahl, Republican, was reelected to a third term.

1949   Theodore Roosevelt National Memorial Park was dedicated June 4.

1950   Korean War, 1950-1953. C. Norman Brunsdale, Republican, was elected governor. State population only 619,636.

1951   Oil was discovered near Tioga in April.

1952   The second largest farm production year on record in North Dakota. Brunsdale was reelected governor.

1953   President Dwight Eisenhower spoke at the closure ceremonies at the Garrison Dam. A new oil field was discovered in Billings County. The first television stations in the state began broadcasting, KCJB-TV Minot, WDAY-TV Fargo, and KFYR-TV Bismarck.

1954   The first large oil refinery in North Dakota was dedicated at Mandan October 2. Brunsdale was reelected to a third term as governor.

1956   John E. Davis, Republican, was elected governor. The Nonpartisan League and the Democratic party merged to form the Democratic/NPL party. Contracts let for construction of the interstate highway system. Construction began at Grand Forks Air Force Base. Mary College established at Bismarck.

1957   Construction began at Minot Air Force Base.

1958 The Theodore Roosevelt drama "Old Four Eyes" opened at the Burning Hills Amphitheater near Medora. Quentin Burdick elected to the U.S. House of Representatives. Gov. John E. Davis reelected to a second term.

1959 The outdoor drama "Trails West" depicting the life of Gen. George Custer in the west opened at Fort Lincoln State Park near Mandan. William Langer, colorful political figure and U.S. Senator, died November 8. A.C. Townley, founder of the Nonpartisan League died. Foundation Aid Program for state aid to public schools was established.

1960 William L. Guy, Democrat, elected governor. Quentin Burdick elected to the U.S. Senate. Commercial salt production began in North Dakota. North Dakota Agricultural College was renamed the North Dakota State University of Agriculture and Applied Science. State population climbed to 632,446.

1961 Thirty-seventh Legislative Assembly named John Burke, North Dakota statesman, to one of two places alloted the state in the National Statuary Hall at Washington, D.C., and authorized the Dakota Territory Centennial Commission. Thirty-two counties were declared a drought disaster area by Secretary of Agriculture Orville Freeman. The North Dakota School for the Blind, in operation since 1908 at Bathgate, was reestablished at Grand Forks.

1962 Gov. William Guy reelected to a second term.

1963 Statue of John Burke, former governor and Supreme Court justice of North Dakota and treasurer of the United States, was placed in Statuary Hall of the Capitol in Washington. Voters in referendum election defeated new tax measures enacted by 1963 state legislature. Republican Mark Andrews won the special election to fill the unexpired term of the late United States Representative Hjalmer Nygaard.

1964 Gov. William Guy reelected to a third term. Rolland Redlin, Democrat, replaced Don Short, and Mark Andrews was elected to the United States House of Representatives. The Minot Minuteman Missile complex was declared operational.

1965 The Omnibus Tax measure, passed by the 1965 state legislature, was defeated in a special referendum election. Congress authorized the Garrison Diversion Reclamation project in North Dakota. Quentin Burdick was reelected to the United States Senate. Funding for the Garrison Diversion Project approved by Congress. Democrats controlled the state House of Representatives for the first time.

1966 A blizzard, called the worst in history by the Chicago Weather Bureau, struck much of the state. The Red River crested at 45.63 feet at Grand Forks in a flood termed the worst of the twentieth century. Honorable Fred Aandahl, former governor, died April 7. The former State College at Ellendale became a branch of the University of North Dakota. Former Gov. John Davis elected National Commander of the American Legion. Mark Andrews was reelected to Congress.

1967 Cornerstone of the new $2.3 million State Highway Department building laid. Fortieth State Legislature went into overtime session as Gov. William Guy vetoed an unprecedented number of its actions. North Dakota transferred the site of old Fort Union to the National Park Service.

1968 Gov. William Guy reelected to an unprecedented fourth term. Milton R. Young was reelected United States Senator, and Mark Andrews and Tom Kleppe were reelected as United States Representatives. A mild earthquake, first to be known in North Dakota, was felt in the Bismarck area.

1969 The State Legislature repealed the personal property tax, replacing it with a broadened sales tax base, and increased the sales tax to 4 percent. Deep snow accumulations and storms caused numerous lengthy school closings over the state and resulted in extreme floods, especially in the Minot area. Fire destroys the State Mill and Elevator in Grand Forks. A "Zip to Zap" party attended by thousands of young people left only minor damage in Zap, North Dakota.

1970 ABM missile installation began construction near Nekoma; the facility was completed in 1974, but closed several months later. Construction initiated on the McClusky Canal. State population dips to 617,761.

1971 State Constitutional Convention convened. Constitution crafted by the Convention was defeated by voters in 1972.

1972 Arthur Link elected to his first term as governor.

1973 Record high grain prices boosted the North Dakota economy.

1974 Incumbent Senator Milton Young defeated William Guy in the closest U.S. Senate race in state history. Arthur Link reelected governor.

1975   North Dakota ratified the Equal Rights
        Amendment.

1976   Groundbreaking for the North Dakota
        Heritage Center.

1977   Last section of Interstate 29 completed,
        thus making North Dakota the first state
        to finish its interstate highway system.

1978   Sunflowers became the state's second-
        largest cash crop. Oil boom began in
        western North Dakota.

1979   Coal Creek power station went "on-line."

1980   Allen Olson elected governor. Great
        Plains Coal Gasification Plant construc-
        tion began. State population rose to
        652,717.

1981   North Dakota Heritage Center opened.

1982   Quentin Burdick reelected to the
        U.S. Senate.

1983   Longest legislative session in history
        ended.

1984   Great Plains Coal Gasification Plant com-
        pleted. George Sinner elected Governor.

1985   Great Plains Coal Gasification Associates
        defaulted on a federal loan; U.S. Depart-
        ment of Energy assumed control of the
        Great Plains Coal Gasification Plant.

1986   Kent Conrad defeated Republican Mark
        Andrews for a seat in the U.S. Senate.

1987   State population estimated at 685,000.

Northorth Dakota has changed tremendously over the past 100 years. Some of these changes took a great deal of courage and wisdom to see into the future. Other changes came as a natural part of growth. Every change worked toward preserving the ideals of our state and country.

"A state without the means of some change is without the means of its conservation."

—EDMUND BURKE

First National Corporation, consisting of First National Bank, Northwood State Bank and West Fargo State Bank has its roots in over 50 years of growth. But one thing has remained the same—the commitment of secure financial planning for family and business. And the ability to think in the long-term.

First National Corporation applauds our state and the people who had the foresight to expect and welcome change. We're proud to perpetuate that quality in our everyday business.

Every Year Gets Brighter!

Celebrating North Dakota

KXJB-TV ④
RED RIVER VALLEY

SOURCES

The sources of information for a book such as this are many, varied, and somewhat different from a more conventional history. As individuals who work with the interpretation of North Dakota's history on a daily basis, the authors find themselves drawing upon certain standard works regularly. Included among these are Elwyn B. Robinson, *History of North Dakota* (Lincoln: University of Nebraska Press, 1966); Robert P. and Wynona H. Wilkins, *North Dakota: A History* (New York: W. W. Norton and Company, 1977); D. Jerome Tweton and Theodore B. Jelliff, *North Dakota: The Heritage of a People* (Fargo: Institute for Regional Studies, 1976); Theodore B. Jelliff, *North Dakota: A Living Legacy* (Fargo: K and K Publishers, 1983); *North Dakota: A Guide to the Northern Prairie State* (Fargo: Knight Printing Company, 1938); C. L. Dill, *Early Peoples of North Dakota* (Bismarck: State Historical Society of North Dakota, 1983); and Mary Jane Schneider, *North Dakota Indians: An Introduction,* (Dubuque: Kendall Hunt, 1986). The authors also drew upon numerous articles in *North Dakota History,* and for the early settlement period *The Record,* Clement Lounsberry's turn-of-the-century effort to combine history and boosterism.

The many primary sources available at the State Historical Society of North Dakota were also used in compiling this book. Most noteworthy are the photographic collections which have been credited. In addition, the vast newspaper holdings, state government records, and manuscript collections yielded information of interest. Print collections and reference works such as *Polk* city directories, county histories, *North Dakota Blue Books,* and *Who's Who in North Dakota,* were also consulted. The authors benefited from overviews and interpretive items, both published and unpublished, which have been developed to interpret the history of North Dakota to the public.

For those interested in further reading in North Dakota history, *Reference Guide to North Dakota History and North Dakota Literature* (Grand Forks: University of North Dakota, 1979), by Dan Rylance and J. F. S. Smeall, provides a comprehensive listing of published sources. Two journals are currently published that provide articles of interest on a broad range of subjects relating to the state's history, *North Dakota History,* published by the State Historical Society of North Dakota, and *North Dakota Quarterly,* published by the University of North Dakota.

A

A-na-shi-u, 44
Aandahl, Fred G., 162, 163, 168, 170, 253, 254
Abortion, 215
Accounts and Purchases, Dept. of, 171
Agricultural processing industries, 187, 192
Airlines, 204
Alcoholism, 123
Alexander, 210
Alfalfa, 156
Allin, Roger, 83, 252
Allotment Act, 29, 45
Ambrose, Fr., 41
Amenia, 210
Amerada Oil Company, 165, 175
America First Committee, 159
American Crystal Sugar Company, 192
American elm, 232
American Fur Company, 50, 51, 53, 54, 250
Amidon, Charles F., 129
Amoco Oil Company, 192
Amoco Oil Refinery, 175
Andrews, Mark, 194, 195, 254, 255
Anson Northrop, 54, 250
Antelope, 176
Anti-garb measure, 169
Anti-missile missiles, 194, 254
Arapahoe Indians, 19
Archaic Indians, 17
Arikara Indians, 21-25, 30, 53, 249, 250
Arvilla, 102
Ashley, W. H., 249
Aspen, 5
Assiniboine Indians, 19, 24, 27, 28, 51, 53
Assiniboine River, 49
Astoria Overland Expedition, 249
Atkinson, Henry, 250
Atkinson-O'Fallon Expedition, 249
Atlatls, 17
Auctions, 216
Audubon, John James, 250
Auger, Joseph J., 104
Automobiles, 107, 121, 133, 135, 137, 139, 160, 163, 177, 185, 188, 201, 203, 215

B

B-52, 198
B. H. Smith Wagon Shop and Blacksmithing, 107
Bad Gun, 28
Badlands, 12, 14, 15, 17, 119, 165
Baer, John, 133
Bailey, Robert, 101
Baker, Berta, 171, 181
Baker, Stephen A., 65
Bands, 71
Bank of North Dakota, 129, 134, 252
Banks, 104, 146, 251
Baptist Church, 55, 127, 144, 145
Barley, 163, 253
Barnard, Alonzo, 250
Baseball, 72, 118, 126
Basin Electric Power Cooperative, 210
Basset, Arthur, 252
Bathgate, 104, 254

Bathgate Dakota Bank, 104
Battle of Big Mound, 54, 250
Battle of Dead Buffalo Lake, 54, 250
Battle of Killdeer Mountains, 59, 250
Battle of Stony Lake, 54, 250
Battle of the Little Big Horn, 42, 57, 64, 66, 251
Battle of Whitestone Hill, 59, 250
Battle of Wounded Knee, 57, 75, 80
Beach, 92
Beans, 187
Beef Commission, 195
Belcourt, 47, 192
Belcourt, George, 250
Berlin, 163
Berry-Boise Cattle Company, 113
Berthold, 93
Berthold, Bartholomew, 250
Beulah, 160, 188, 201, 214
Bicycles, 116, 121
Big Foot, 57, 75
Bihrle, Craig, 7, 15, 230
Billings County, 165
Bismarck, 64, 65, 79, 80, 82-87, 126, 137, 140, 162, 163, 168, 174, 178, 183, 188, 189, 194, 197, 201, 203, 212, 222, 241, 251-254
Bismarck High School, 184
Bismarck Indian Boarding School, 29, 35
Bismarck Tribune, 251
Bisons (NDSU), 229
Black Buffalo, 24
Black Hills, 83, 251
Black Hills Expedition, 57, 65, 82, 251
Black military units, 62
Blackfoot Indians, 19, 35, 50, 51, 54
Blacks, 62, 145, 249
Blacksmiths, 107
Blind pigs, 122
Blizzards, 209, 253, 254
Bobcat loader, 222
Bodmer, Karl, 22, 23, 25, 37
Bois de Sioux, 13, 14
Boller, Henry, 54
Bonanza farms, 85, 90, 251
Bonza, Pierre, 249
Bottineau, 126, 135, 252
Bottineau County, 80, 165, 251
Bouga, William, 45
Bowman, 105, 118
Bozeman Trail, 55
Bradbury, John, 249
Bradley, Robert, 199
Bridges, 137
Briggs, Frank, 117, 252
Brossert, Marv, 224
Brown, George D., 116
Brunsdale, C. Norman, 163, 164, 170, 174, 253
Bry, Edward, 14, 232, 233, 238, 245
Bryan, William Jennings, 91
Buffalo, 14, 51, 53, 56-58
Buffalo Bill Wild West Show, 73
Buffalo bones, 94
Bull boats, 22, 53
Bullhead, Henry, 74
Burdick Collection, 21

Burdick, Quentin, 170, 180, 194, 197, 254, 255
Burdick, Usher, 94, 168, 170, 171, 197
Burke County, 165
Burke, Andrew, 252
Burke, John, 91, 129, 252, 254
Burleigh County, 87, 128, 251
Burlington Subsistence Homestead Project, 153
Bus lines, 252
Butchering, 96
Butte, 216
Buttes, 10

C

CENEX, 168
Civil Works Administration, 154
Cabin courts, 137
Cameron, John, 249
Camp Greeley (Camp Hancock), 80
Camp Hancock, 64, 80, 251
Canadian Pacific Railroad, 79
Cando, 192
Cannonball River, 16, 21, 60
Capitol Commission, 79, 87
Carlsen, Anne, 193
Carpenter's Union, 183
Carrington, 156
Carver, Jonathon, 249
Case, Harold, 32
Cass County, 148, 251
Cass-Cheney Farm, 90
Casselton, 79
Cathedral Car, 127
Catholic Church, 29, 32, 47, 55, 127, 144, 169, 181, 217, 249, 252
Catlin, George, 37, 250
Cattle, 109, 187, 216, 218
Cavalier County, 251
Cavileer, Charles, 77, 78, 250
Centennial Commission, 210
Central Waterfowl Flyway, 230
Chaboillez, Charles, 55, 249
Chaloner, William, 137
Chardon, Francis, 53
Chautauqua, 120, 121
Cheese, 229
Cheyenne Indians, 19, 23, 27, 28
Chickens, 187
Children, 125, 203
Chippewa Indians, 19, 21, 22, 24, 27-29, 35, 44, 46, 47, 57, 251
Chronology, 249
Church of the Brethren, 97
Clark Equipment Company, 222
Climate, 17
Coal, 126, 127, 163, 187, 188, 193, 201, 214, 229, 251
Coal Creek Power Plant, 223
Coal mining, 145, 146, 168, 192, 223
Cody, William F., 73
Colonies of settlers, 97
Columbia Fur Company, 249-250
Committee for Progressive Unity, 168
Congregational Church, 29, 32, 55, 127, 144
Conrad, Kent, 195, 255

Constitutional Convention, 80, 87, 194, 254
Continental Divide, 13
Cooke, Jay, 78
Cooperatives, 93, 117, 135, 163, 170
Crazy Bull, 28
Creameries, 108
Cree Indians, 24, 27-28, 51
Crippled Children's School, 193
Crosby, 132, 164
Crow Indians, 19, 21, 27-28, 51, 54
Crunelle, Leonard, 246
Custer Drama, 202
Custer, Elizabeth, 65
Custer, George A., 57, 65, 82, 251, 254

D
d'Eglise, Jacques, 249
Dahl, C. P., 194
Dairy Princess, 174
Dairy Products Promotion Commission, 195
Dakota Indians, 19, 23
Dakota Territory, 77, 250
Dakota Territory Centennial Commission,
    254
Dalager, John, 165
Dalrymple Farm, 90
Davies, Ronald, 177
Davis, Charles P., 117
Davis, John, 170-171, 174, 180, 197, 253-254
De Smet, Jean, 55, 250-251
Deadwood, 82
Democratic party, 129, 151-152, 162, 168,
    170, 180, 194, 197, 210, 252-253
Derby, James F., 104
Devils Lake, 5, 15, 19, 21, 54-55, 64, 77, 79-80,
    120-122, 140, 144, 252
Devine, Joseph M., 252
Dickinson, 58, 114, 117, 126, 135, 181,
    183, 194
Dickinson Normal School, 252
Dorgan, Byron, 194
Drayton, 192, 198
Drift Prairie, 7, 14-16
Drought, 83, 134, 147, 149, 252-253
Dry Edible Bean Council, 195
Dumoulin, Severe J., 249
Dunn County, 10
Durum, 253

E
Early Prehistoric Period, 17
Earth mover, 170
Earthquakes, 254
Economic Development Commission,
    171, 243
Edge, William, 249
Eilson, Carl Ben, 142
Eisenhuth, Laura J., 252
Electric plants, 168
Electrical power, 193, 223, 227
Electrification, 163
Elk, 5
Elkhorn Ranch, 110, 165
Ellendale, 80
Ellendale Normal School, 126, 252, 254
Elm River, 14
Enderlin, 227
Energy development, 165, 187-188
Episcopal Church, 127
Equal Rights Amendment, 255
Equity Cooperative Exchange, 135
Exploration, 49

F
Federal Emergency Relief Administration,
    152, 154

Fairs, 118, 208
Family farms, 218
Fancher, Fred B., 252
Far West, 66-67
Fargo, 79-81, 84-85, 109, 115, 126, 140, 154,
    167, 168, 177, 181-182, 208, 215, 222, 224-
    225, 251-252
Fargo Express, 251
Fairbanks, Avard, 247
Farm Holiday Association, 148
Farm size, 89
Farm economy, 133
Farm income, 187, 203
Farm surpluses, 163
Farmers Union Progressive Alliance, 168
Farmers Union Terminal Association, 135
Ferries, 137
Fire departments, 116
Fires, 115, 154, 206
First American Banks of North Dakota, 2
Fisher's Landing, 77
Fishing, 189
Fisk, James L., 250
Fiske, Frank B., 43, 104
Flasher Public School, 100
Flax, 92
Flickertail, 245
Flickertail State, 245
Flickertail, The, 240
Flood control, 171, 173
Floods, 106, 254
Flour mills, 108, 192
Foley, James W., 240
Football, 229
Forest River, 14, 249
Forman, 119
Fort Abercrombie, 54-55, 57-58, 70, 77,
    250-251
Fort Abraham Lincoln, 55, 57, 64-65, 67, 70,
    202, 251-252
Fort Atkinson, 54
Fort Berthold, 53, 60
Fort Berthold Indian Reservation, 26-27, 29,
    31-33, 164, 251
Fort Buford, 55, 57, 62-63, 72, 250-252
Fort Clark, 22, 53, 250
Fort Cross (Fort Seward), 80
Fort Dilts, 250
Fort Floyd, 250
Fort Kipp, 250
Fort Laramie Treaty, 54-55, 57, 251
Fort Lincoln, 131, 162-163, 252
Fort Lincoln State Park, 254
Fort Mandan, 249
Fort Manuel Lisa, 50, 249
Fort McKeen, 64, 67, 251
Fort Pembina, 55, 57, 71, 251-252
Fort Ransom, 55, 250-251
Fort Rice, 55, 57, 60, 250-251
Fort Seward, 55, 57, 80, 251
Fort Stevenson, 55, 57, 63, 66, 251
Fort Tilton, 249
Fort Totten, 35, 55, 57, 64, 75, 251-252
Fort Totten Indian Boarding School, 29
Fort Totten Indian Reservation, 29, 32,
    45, 251
Fort Totten Indian School, 75
Fort Union, 51, 60, 63, 250, 254
Fort Yates, 35, 39-40, 44, 68, 71-72, 75, 104,
    131, 156, 251-252
Fort Yates Indian Boarding School, 42
Foster County, 251
Foundation Aid Program, 185, 163, 254
4-H, 156
Frazier, Lynn, 129, 134, 252

Freight House, 85
Fremont, John C., 250
French and Indian War, 49
Frikirke Bygget, 127
Frontier Scout, 60, 250
Fuchs, Norman, 212
Fur trade, 48-53, 55

G
Gall, 42
Galt, Sterling, 117
Gamache School, 126
Gambling, 183, 195
Garreau, Pierre, 27
Garrison Dam, 17, 32, 164, 170-171, 173-174,
    189, 226, 253
Garrison Diversion Project, 165, 193-194,
    209, 226, 254
Gasoline rationing, 160
Gayton, John, 43
Geier, Christ, 96
Geographic Center of North America,
    13, 248
Georgetown, 77
Ghost Dance, 40, 57, 74, 252
Gillen Construction Company, 137
Gingras Trading Post, 48
Gingras, Antoine, 48, 250
Glaciation, 13, 15-16
Gladstone Hotel, 206
Gold Rush, 53-54, 57-58, 65-66, 82, 250-251
Goose Lake, 144
Goose River, 14
Governmental Survey Commission, 171
Governmental reorganization, 171,
    194-195, 210
Governor's Coat of Arms, 235
Grace, Richard V., 161
Grafton, 79, 252
Grafton State School, 252
Grain Terminal Association, 168
Grain trade, 80
Grain elevators, 92, 216
Grain moratorium, 253
Grand Forks, 77, 79, 80, 84, 106, 109, 126,
    140, 161, 205, 208, 222, 249, 251, 254
Grand Forks Air Force Base, 165, 194, 198,
    217, 253
Grand Theatre, 140
Grandin, 251
Grant, Ulysses S., 80, 86
Granville, 109
Grasshoppers, 134, 147-148, 249
Gray, David, 10, 217, 264
Graybear, Henry, 44
Great Dakota Boom, 251
Great Depression, 134, 146-148, 159, 187
Great Northern Railway, 80-81, 94, 97, 102,
    251
Great Plains Coal Gasification Project, 188,
    214, 255
Great Seal of North Dakota, 234
Greater North Dakota Association, 168
Green, Sheldon, 218, 219, 222
Greenough, Marjorie, 163
Griggs, Alexander, 84, 251
Guy, William, 171, 194-195, 199, 210,
    212, 254

H
Hackney-Boyton Land Company, 97
Hagan, Bruce, 194
Hagen, John, 129, 134
Hail Insurance Fund, 252
Halcrow, Don, 194

Hall, Charles L., 32
Hanna, L. B., 252
Harvesting, 192
Harvey, 137
Hatton, 142
Haugland, Brynhild, 215
Hay, 92
Hayes, Charles, 43
Hazelton High School, 202
Hazen, 160
Heart River, 16, 21
Heerman, Edward E., 120
Henry, Alexander, 14, 24, 50, 249
Henry, Andrew, 249
Herons, 15, 230
Hersey, Dudley H., 102
Hidatsa Indians, 19-22, 24-26, 28, 30-31,
    53, 250
Higher education, 126, 205
Highway Department, State, 139, 252, 254
Highway Patrol, 139
Hill, James J., 78, 84, 251
Hillsboro, 106
Hillsboro Fire Department, 116
Hillside Park Pool, 188
Historical Society, State, 164, 193, 211,
    243, 252
Hjelle, Walt, 199
Holmboe, Frithjof, 140
Holmes, Thomas A., 250
Homesteading, 77, 95, 97, 111, 113-114,
    250-251
Honey, 187
Horses, 94
Hospital for the Insane, 80, 251
Hospitals, 222
Hudson's Bay Company, 49, 77, 249-250
Hughes and Hersey Lumberyard, 102
Hughes, Frank D., 102
Huidekoper, A. C., 111, 113
Hunters, 56
Hunting, 119, 176
Huse, Carter, 62
Hydroelectric power, 164-165, 171, 173

I
I-29, 199, 255
I-94, 180, 199
ICBM, 165, 194, 217, 254
Immigration, 77-78, 79-80, 83, 127
Independent Voters Association, 129, 133
    134, 252-253
Indian Boarding Schools, 29, 33, 35
Indian Police, 28, 40, 44, 74
Indian Reorganization Act, 29
Indian Self-Determination and Educational
    Assistance Act, 29
Indian Wars, 55
Industrial Commission, 134, 252
Industrial School, 80
Insurance Commission, 164
Insurgents, 170
International Peace Garden, 244
Interstate Highway System, 165, 180, 188,
    199, 253, 255
Iowa Indians, 23
Iowa Territory, 250
Irrigation, 153, 156, 164, 193, 209, 226
Isolationism, 159
Iverson, Clarence, 165, 175

J
Jacobsen, Martin, 135
James River, 16
Jamestown, 78-80, 96, 108, 135, 137, 149-150,
    168, 180, 192-193, 206, 251
Jamestown College, 251
Jayne, William, 250
Jesseaume, Rene, 249
J. L. Grandin, 85
Johnson Land and Cattle Company, 92
Johnson, Lyndon B., 197

K
KBOM, 140
KCJB-TV, 168, 253
KDLR, 140
KFJM, 140
KFYR, 140
KFYR-TV, 168, 174, 253
KGCU, 140
KPLM, 140
KXMA-TV, 1
KXMB-TV, 1
KXMC-TV, 1
KXMD-TV, 1
Keeley Institute of Fargo, 123
Kenel, Fr. Martin, 41
Kennedy, John F., 187, 193
Kidder County, 251
Killdeer Mountains, 10, 17
Kinney, John F., 217
Kipp's Post, 250
Kipp, James, 249-250
Kirkwood Mall, 225
Kittson, Norman, 55, 250
Klaus, Anton, 206
Kleppe, Thomas, 254
Knife River, 16, 21-22, 24, 50, 249
Knife River Coal Company, 201
Knutson, Robert, 219
Korean War, 163, 187, 194, 253
Krem Creamery, 108
Krem Roller Mill, 108
Krueger, Otto, 164
Kulm, 86

L
La Salle, 249
La Verendrye, 19, 21, 49, 235, 249
Lalonde, Mike, 241
LaMoure County, 251
Labor, 127, 133, 146, 150, 168, 183, 200, 251
Labor, Department of, 195
Ladd, Edwin, 129, 253
Lake Agassiz, 4, 14
Lake Oahe, 17
Lake Sakakawea, 13, 17, 164, 171, 194,
    226, 238
Lake Souris Plain, 15
Lakota Indians, 23
Land surveyors, 95
Land companies, 100, 126
Langdon, 79
Langer, Lydia, 150
Langer, William, 134-135, 150, 152, 162, 168,
    170, 174, 253-254
Larimore, 79
Late Prehistoric Period, 18-19
Le Raye, Charles, 249
Le Sueur, Arthur, 252
Leader, The, 133
Leavenworth, Henry, 249-250
Legislative Assembly, 87, 129, 132, 171, 185,
    215, 232-233, 235-236, 238, 240
Legislative Research Committee, 171
Leith, 152
Lemke, William, 129, 134, 171, 253
Lewis and Clark Bridge, 137
Lewis and Clark Expedition, 21, 28, 31, 50,
    126, 246, 249
Lewis, Meriwether, 50
Libby, Orin G., 164
Liberty Loan, 129
Liberty Memorial Bridge, 137
Liberty Memorial Building, 149, 241, 243
Libraries, 252
Library Commission, State, 133
Library, State, 243
Lignite, 165
Like-A-Fishhook-Village, 22, 25, 53
Link, Arthur A., 194, 210-211, 254
Linton, 96, 153
Lisa, Manuel, 50-51, 249
Lisbon, 80
Litchville, 162
Little Crow, 250
Little Missouri Horse Company, 111
Lilttle Missouri River, 16-17, 110, 137
Logan County, 251
Lonetree Reservoir, 194
Long Knife, 24
Long, Stephen H., 249
Longfellow, D. W., 27
Louisiana Purchase, 249
Louisiana Territory, 49-50, 249
Lounsberry, C. A., 251
Lutheran Church, 144, 217
Lynx, 16

M
MacLeod, Bob, 174
Maddock, Walter, 253
Mallberg, Leon, 194
Maltese Cross Ranch, 110
Mandan, 80, 118, 140, 163, 165, 168, 175, 183,
    192, 253-254
Mandan Development Association, 202
Mandan Indians, 19, 21-24, 26-28, 30, 49-50,
    53-54, 249-250
Manufacturing, 108-109, 168, 187-188,
    192, 222
Many Bears, 30
Mapleton, 195
Marquis de Mores, 111-112, 118, 251
Marsh, Grant, 66
Marty, Martin (Abbot), 41
Mary College, 253
Maximilian, 250
Mayville, 79-80, 126
Mayville Normal School, 252
McCabe Methodist Church, 183
McCarney, Robert, 189, 194
McClusky, 180
McClusky Canal, 194, 254
McCreary, Ida, 156
McGregor, 165
McHenry County, 80, 109, 122, 147, 251
McIntosh County, 125
McKenzie County, 137, 156, 165
McKenzie, Alexander, 80, 87, 91
McKenzie, Kenneth, 250
McLean County, 216
McLean, Harry F., 247
McLean, John A., 65
McLeod, John, 249
Medina, 97
Medora, 83, 111-113, 165, 251, 254
Meier, Ben, 176
Melroe Division, 222
Mercer County, 212
Methodist Church, 127, 144, 183
Metis, 24, 29, 51, 56-57
Meyer Broadcasting Company, 174
Meyer, Etta, 174

Michigan, 125
Middle Prehistoric Period, 17
Middle Woodland Period, 19
Midland Continental Railroad Company, 168
Migrant workers, 200
Milk, 108, 187, 218, 240
Mill and Elevator Association, 129, 134, 252, 254
Miller, Bob, 126
Miller, John, 80, 252
Mineral industries, 219
Mink Woman, 31
Minnesota Massacre, 54
Minnie H., 120
Minot, 79, 94, 126, 135, 140, 145, 168, 215, 253-254
Minot Air Force Base, 165, 194, 198, 217, 253
Minot State College, 215, 252
Missionaries, 32, 250
Missouri Breaks, 16
Missouri Company, 249
Missouri Escarpment, 15-16
Missouri Fur Company, 50, 249
Missouri Plateau, 16, 83
Missouri River, 4, 13-17, 19, 21-23, 25, 28, 51, 54-55, 63-64, 77, 79, 81-82, 85, 164, 170-171, 193-194, 209, 226, 249-250, 253
Missouri River Diversion Association, 144
Missouri Slope, 109, 111
Missouri Territory, 249
Missouri-Souris Diversion Unit, 164
Mohall, 86, 140, 161, 164
Moodie, Thomas, 151-152, 253
Moorhead, 81
Morris, W. C., 133
Morton County, 100, 134, 208
Moses, John, 152, 160, 162-163, 168, 253
Motion pictures, 140
Mott, 99, 105
Mountrail County, 165, 251
Mouse River, 24, 126, 194, 249
Muench, Aloisius, 181
Music, 71, 178, 184, 186, 222

N

Nakota Indians, 23
Napoleon, 176
National Farmers Union, 135
National Guard, 117, 128, 150, 163, 212, 252
National Sun Industries, 227
Natural gas, 188, 192, 214, 219
Neche, 79
Nekoma, 194
Nelson County, 125
Nestos, R. A., 134, 252
New England, 118
Newborg, Gerald, 264
Newspapers, 60, 86, 109, 133, 168, 178, 205, 224, 250-251
Nicollet, Jean N., 250
NoDak Mutual Insurance Company, 168
Nonpartisan League, 93, 129, 132-135, 151, 162, 168, 170, 252-254
Noodles by Leonardo, 192
Normal schools, 126
North Dakota Agricultural College, 80, 126, 129, 240, 252
North Dakota Capitol, 87
North Dakota Farm Bureau, 168, 253
North Dakota Farmers' Union, 135, 149, 168, 170, 253
North Dakota Heritage Center, 211, 241, 243, 255
North Dakota Hymn, 240
North Dakota State University, 229, 254

North Dakota Wheat Growers Association, 135
Northern Pacific Railroad, 64, 77-79, 80-84, 86-87, 90, 97, 109, 134, 199, 251
Northern pike, 238
Northwest Airlines, 204
North West Company, 50, 249
Nuttal, Thomas, 249
Nye, Gerald, 135, 159-160, 253
Nygaard, Hjalmer, 254

O

Oahe Dam, 7
Oak, 5
Oakes, 92
Oats, 229
Office of Management and Budget, 195
Oil, 163, 165, 175, 187, 192, 219, 252-253, 255
Oil refineries, 165, 175, 192, 253
Old Four Eyes, 254
Old Guard, 170
Olson, Allen, 194, 210, 255
Olson, Ole, 151, 253
One Bull, 40
Opera houses, 119
Otoe Indians, 23
Otter Trail Power Company, 145, 227
Owens, John, 217

P

Paleo-Indians, 17
Panic of 1873, 78
Park River, 14, 79, 156, 249
Park River Post, 50
Peace Garden State, 244
Pembina, 24, 50, 55, 57, 77, 249-250
Pembina County, 80, 251
Pembina Hills, 14
Pembina River, 14, 50
Pendroy family, 122
Penitentiary, 80, 251
Percheron horses, 94
Personal property tax, 254
Photography, 43
Physicians, 222
Pick-Sloan Plan, 164, 170-171, 253
Picnics, 118, 132
Pierce County, 248
Pioneer family statue, 247
Pipelines, 165, 175
Plains Village People, 19
Ployhar, James D., 240
Police departments, 116
Politics, 83, 86-87, 91, 93, 129, 132-135, 149-152, 160, 162-163, 168, 170, 174, 176, 189, 194-195, 197, 210, 252-254
Popcorn wagon, 140
Pope, Ted, 102
Population, 29, 78-79, 83-84, 108, 115, 134, 145, 163, 168, 178, 188, 205, 216, 224, 251-252, 254-255
Populists, 93, 252
Post Trader, 70
Post offices, 250
Potato Council, 195
Potatoes, 93, 229, 253
Pow-wows, 224
Prairie Chicken, 28
Prairie dogs, 16-17
Pratt, Richard Henry, 29
Presbyterian Church, 127, 144
Progressives, 129
Prohibition, 122, 252-253
Provencher, Joseph, 249

Public Instruction, Superintendent of, 252
Putnam, C. S., 240

Q

Quality of life, 203
Quilting party, 122

R

ROC, 162, 168, 253
Radio stations, 140, 168, 178, 195, 224, 252
Railroad mileage, 79, 83
Railroads, 53-54, 77-82, 83, 86, 93-94, 97, 120-121, 127, 165, 168, 188, 205, 250-252
Ramsey County, 97, 251
Ranching, 109-114, 218, 221, 251
Ransom County, 251
Recall, 252
Recreation, 5, 72, 116, 118-122, 126, 140, 164, 171, 176, 188-189, 193, 202, 208, 226, 229
Red Buffalo Cow, 28
Red River of the North, 13, 24, 54-55, 58, 77, 84, 106, 194, 205, 249-250
Red River cart, 24, 56, 250
Red River Valley, 3-4, 14-15, 48, 50, 53, 77, 79, 83, 91, 106, 187-188, 251, 253
Redlin, Rolland, 254
Reform School, 80
Reineke, Earl C., 140
Reiten Television, Inc., 1
Renville County, 251
Republican party, 129, 134, 150-152, 162, 168, 170, 174, 176, 180, 189, 194-195, 252-253
Retailers, 192, 215, 225
Richardson ground squirrel, 245
Richland County, 127, 251
Riel, Louis, 53
Riverdale, 171
Roads, 136-137, 180
Robinson, Elwyn B., 80
Rock Lake, 107
Rocky Mountain Fur Company, 249
Rodeos, 118, 163
Rolette County, 80, 251
Rolette, Joseph, 77, 250-251
Roosevelt, Franklin, 144, 159
Roosevelt, Theodore, 110, 251, 254
Roseglen, 128
Roseglen State Bank, 146
Rosser, Thomas L., 79
Rosten, Harry, 128
Roughnecks, 219
Roy's Post, 249
Rugby, 248
Russian Baptist Conference, 144

S

Sahnish, 21
Saint Joseph, 77
Saint Paul and Pacific Railroad, 77-78
Saint Paul, Minneapolis, and Manitoba Railroad, 79, 84, 94
Saint Peters, 53
Saint Thomas, 79
Sakakawea, 31, 246, 249
Salt, 199, 254
Salt River, 249
Sarles, E. Y., 252
Sauger, 189
Scaffold burial, 37
School for the Blind, 80, 254
School for the Deaf, 80, 252
School of Forestry, 80, 126, 252
School of Science, 80, 126, 252
Schools, 29, 33, 35, 47, 75, 100, 123, 125-126,

163, 177, 184-185, 188, 202, 223, 249, 253-254
ranton Fire Department, 116
cond Baptist Church, 145
lkirk, 249
lkirk, 84
ntinel Butte, 176
afer, George, 253
anley, John, 127
eep, 114
eridan County, 251
eyenne, 86
eyenne Blizzard, 86
eyenne River, 14, 55
eyenne Township, 127
opping malls, 215, 225
ort, Don, 195, 254
ortridge, Eli C. D., 83, 252
oley, Henry H., 54, 250
nner, George, 194, 255
oux Indians, 19, 21-24, 28, 35, 37, 39-40, 42-43, 54-55, 57, 59, 66, 72, 75, 131, 249-252
oux Uprising, 250
oux War of 1876, 57
tting Bull, 40, 57, 72-75, 80, 251-252
aughterhouses, 108
ope Region, 9, 11-12, 14, 16, 102, 135
oughs, 15
nallpox, 21-22, 53, 250
ocialist party, 252
od houses, 96, 101
il conservation, 163
il erosion, 147, 156
oldiers, 57, 62, 64, 66, 68, 70-72, 84, 131, 140
oldiers' Home, 80
orlie, Arthur G., 252-253
oybeans, 163
panish-American War, 117, 235, 252
pear, John, 45
pencer David, 55
perry, James E., 7, 211
potted Weasel, 30
t. Joseph (Walhalla), 55, 250
tage lines, 77-78, 82
tandard Marketing Act, 135
tandard Oil Company, 165, 175
tanding Rock Indian Reservation, 29, 32, 39, 40, 42-43, 74-75, 131, 251-252
tanding Soldier, Maggie, 44
tar Village, 22, 25
tate Beverage, 240
tate Bird, 233
tate Capitol, 86, 149, 152, 180, 192, 241-242, 253
tate Constitution, 122, 194, 234, 251-253
tate Crest, 235
tate Fish, 238
tate Flag, 235
tate Flower, 236
tate Fossil, 239
tate Grass, 239
tate Highway Building, 241
tate Hospital, 168
tate Song, 240
tate Symbols, 233
tate Tree, 232
tate Water Commission, 135, 253
tatehood movement, 80
teamboats, 66, 77, 82-85, 250
teiger Tractor, Inc., 225
teven's Survey Expedition, 250
tickney, Dorothy, 181
trandemo, Robert, 203
trasburg, 204
trassmeier, Fr. Bernard, 41

Strip mining, 145-146, 168, 193, 201
Stutsman County, 251
Sugar beets, 163, 187, 198, 200, 229
Sully, Alfred, 54, 59-60, 63, 250
Sun Dance, 22, 24, 27, 37, 46
Sunflower Council, 195
Sunflowers, 187, 227, 255
Supreme Court, 151, 253
Sutton, 101
Swedes, 144
Symbols, 233

T
Talbott, Charles C., 149
Tanner, James, 250
Tarpaper shacks, 95
Telegraph, 251
Telephones, 117, 163, 251
Television, 204
Television stations, 168, 174, 182, 195, 224, 253
Temperance, 122
Teredo bored petrified wood, 239
Terry, Alfred H., 251
Terry, Elijah, 55
Theatres, 140, 168, 178
Theodore Roosevelt National Park, 165, 253
Thompson, David, 249
Three Affiliated Tribes, 22, 24, 29
Threshing, 91-92
Tioga, 165, 175, 253
Tolley, 152
Too Much Mistake, 80
Tornados, 182
Totten Trail, 57
Tourism, 164
Towner, 147
Townley, Arthur C., 129, 132, 134, 171, 254
Tractor, 156
Traill County, 125
Trails West, 254
Trinity Swedish Lutheran Church, 144
Trobriand, Philippe Regis de, 63
Trolleys, 126
Truax-Traer Coal Company, 145-146
Turtle Mountain Indian Reservation, 29, 44, 46-47, 251
Turtle Mountain Manufacturing Company, 192
Turtle Mountains, 5, 15, 244, 250
Turtle River, 14
Turtle River Post, 249

U
U.S.S. Grand Forks, 161, 253
U.S.S. North Dakota, 252
Umber, Harold, 7
Underwood, 223
Union Pacific Railroad, 53
University of North Dakota, 80, 126, 193, 205, 251, 254

V
Valley City, 78-80, 117, 126, 176
Valley City Normal School, 252
Van Lishoutseven, Nelson, 99
Velva, 146, 168
Vietnam War, 194
Villard, Henry, 79, 86
Von Hoffman, Medora, 111

W
WDAY, 140, 252
WDAY-TV, 168, 182, 224, 253
Works Progress Administration, 152-154

Wahpeton, 79-80, 117, 126, 252
Wahpeton Indian Boarding School, 29
Wainwright, Samuel A., 57
Walhalla, 250
Walker, W. D., 127
Ward County, 80, 126, 132, 149, 215
Washburn, 85
Washburn Lignite Coal Company, 127, 145
Water, 135, 144, 153, 170-171, 173-174, 194, 209-210, 253
Water Conservation Districts, 135
Watford City, 137, 138
Weddings, 44
Welford, Walter, 152, 253
Welk, Lawrence, 204
Wells County, 251
Wenstrom, Frank, 194
Western Gear, 192
Western meadowlark, 233
Western wheatgrass, 239
Wetlands, 230
Wheat, 83, 85, 90, 92, 133-136, 156, 163, 169, 187-188, 192, 229, 253
Wheat Commission, 195
Whistler, Joseph, N. G., 70
Whistler Expedition, 251
White Bear, 30
White Calf, 31
White Earth, 122, 148
White Earth River Post, 250
White Shield School, 33
White, Edgar, 156
White, Frank, 252
Whitestone Hill, 54
Wild Rice River, 14
Wild prairie rose, 236
Wildfowl, 15, 17
Wilkins, Hubert, 142
William H. Brown Land Company, 100
Williams County, 123, 165
Williams County Farmers Union, 170
Williston, 126, 137, 165, 170, 175, 194, 197, 199, 205
Williston Basin, 16
Williston Graphic, 109
Williston Opera House, 119
Willow City, 148
Wilton, 127
Windbreaks, 156
Winter, 17, 86, 109, 123, 209, 253-254
Wisconsin Territory, 250
Witmer, Samuel T., 104
Women, 30, 33, 39, 46, 100-102, 163, 171, 181, 190, 193, 195, 215, 252
Woodland Peoples, 17-18
Wool production, 114
Workers' Compensation Bureau, 252
World War I, 128-131, 133, 140, 159-160, 243, 252
World War II, 158-163, 169, 180, 187, 194, 253

X
X Y Company, 249

Y
Yankton, 77, 250
Yellowstone, 250
Yellowstone River, 16, 28, 63, 51, 249-250
Young, Milton, 163-164, 168, 170, 194, 210, 253-254
Youth, 156

Z
Zap In, 212, 254

ABOUT THE AUTHORS

Gerald G. Newborg has been North Dakota State Archivist since 1981. He grew up on a farm in the Red River Valley and received his B.A. in history from Concordia College in Moorhead, Minnesota. He has an M.A. in history from the University of North Dakota and an M.B.A. from Ohio State University. Jerry and his wife, Jean, and their daughters, Erica and Annette, reside in Bismarck.

David P. Gray is Deputy State Archivist with the State Archives and Historical Research Library, State Historical Society of North Dakota. Gray also serves as the Diocesan Archivist/Records Manager for the Roman Catholic Diocese of Bismarck. He has a B.A. in history and an M.A. in historical and archival administration from Wright State University, and a Master's in management from the University of Mary. David Gray resides in Bismarck with his wife, Ellen, and their daughters, Aurielle, Regina, and Victoria.